Praise for *How to Give a Speech*

"For your next presentation, put yourself into the hands of Dr. Gary Genard. Under his wise tutelage, you will learn how to put your speech together, and even better, deliver it as a master speechmaker. *How to Give a Speech* is a *tour de force!* It provides you with step-by-step support for everything you need to become a powerful communicator."

— JOHN BALDONI
Author of *Great Communication Secrets of Great Leaders*

"Reading *How to Give a Speech* was an eye-opening experience. I didn't realize there were so many small changes I could make when presenting to sound more appealing—starting with how I said my own name and title! Gary Genard is an outstanding coach and he's written a terrific how-to guide to public speaking. Get this book, and recommend it to your colleagues."

— JODI WHALEN
Marketing Director, The Food Network

"Although I've been a professional speaker for 13 years, I learned valuable lessons from *How to Give a Speech*. Whether you're a rookie or a veteran, Gary Genard's perceptive, accessible book provides all the tools you need to present with confidence."

— ROBERT SPECTOR
International speaker and author of *The Nordstrom Way to Customer Service Excellence*

"An extremely useful resource for anyone who needs to speak in front of groups, large or small. It has helped me speak with more confidence."

— PETER T. SMITH
Region Vice President, The Hertz Corporation

How to Give a Speech has helped me to develop a robust toolbox of speaking techniques. My communication effectiveness has improved significantly as a result of using these methods. I feel even better about my improved self-confidence and focus in knowing how to utilize these tools for any situation requiring effective communication."

— DAVID BEAN
Vice President of Finance, Vertex Pharmaceuticals

"*How to Give a Speech* offers a friendly, engaging roadmap to public speaking. It's an insightful read. Dr. Genard discusses the importance of being honest in your remarks, while maintaining a conversational tone with your audience. *How to Give a Speech* shares invaluable techniques on how to be a successful speaker and presenter."

— LISA MURKOWSKI
U.S. Senator (Alaska)

"These techniques work! As a communicator to global audiences, I have found Dr. Genard's tips extremely helpful in achieving clarity and power, and getting my critical messages out. His techniques for relaxation, visualization, and audience analysis have become common practice for me. From speeches to meetings to conference calls, *How to Give a Speech* is a book that has helped improve my communication skills and reduced my frustrations."

— XIAOWEN HEURTEUX
VP/Senior Financial Analyst, Citigroup

HOW TO
Give a
Speech

Also by Gary Genard

Fearless Speaking: Beat Your Anxiety, Build Your Confidence,
Change Your Life

HOW TO
Give a Speech

EASY-TO-LEARN SKILLS
for Successful Presentations,
Speeches, Pitches, Lectures,
and More!

GARY GENARD

Cedar &
Maitland
Press

How to Give a Speech: Easy-to-Learn Skills for Successful Presentations,
Speeches, Pitches, Lectures, and More! Second expanded edition.

To order this book, please call (617) 993-3410, or write to:

The Genard Method
93 Concord Avenue, Suite 3
Belmont, MA 02478
www.GenardMethod.com
info@GenardMethod.com

Discounts are available for bulk purchases and academic courses.

ISBN: 978-0-9796314-6-7

Library of Congress Control Number: 2016911338

To Janice and Lydia

Acknowledgments

For their suggestions, guidance, and generosity in the preparation of this book, I'd like to thank the following people: John Baldoni, Karma Kitaj, Gretel Hartman, Jodi Whalen, and Christian Koestler. I'd also like to express my heartfelt gratitude to colleagues, friends, and family who gave me advice on the second edition: Arny Bereson, Patty Crowley, Venkat Janapareddy, Avinash Kambadakone, Joe Kvedar, Barry Levin, Brian Morris, Jesus Paez-Cortez, Linda Patch, Carla Reeves, Kirsten Singleton, and my wife Janice and daughter Lydia. And special thanks to Mara Levin, who went beyond the call in providing some timely, and much appreciated advice.

Table of Contents

CHAPTER FIFTEEN: Nuts & Bolts: Practical Skills for Presenters

CHAPTER SIXTEEN: Looking Ahead: The Future of Public Speaking

Preface to the Second Edition

I hope you'll find this book an easy-to-use, practical handbook for enjoyable and successful public speaking. You'll be introduced in these pages to skills based in theatrical techniques in a way meant to be accessible to everyone. Nine years ago when *How to Give a Speech* was first published, the book consisted of 75 "Quick Tips" for more effective speeches and presentations. This format had a simple rationale. As an actor and speech coach, I believed that a hands-on approach inspired by theatrical performance was the best way to improve your ability to speak to audiences—any audiences.

In the years since then, I've added to and refined this method of performance-based public speaking training in my work through The Genard Method. This second expanded edition of *How to Give a Speech* draws upon the continuing lessons I've learned and those I've taught. I'm deeply grateful to my clients, friends, colleagues, and fellow speakers who have been a part of this exciting personal journey.

In this edition, you'll find twenty-six added Quick Tips for a new total of 101 entries, in sixteen chapters rather than the original ten. The six new chapters expand upon information in areas I felt now needed more individual focus. These topics include breathing and relaxation, using PowerPoint and other presentation media, body language, acting techniques for public speaking, how to excel in phone conversations and conference calls, and a glance at what the future of public speaking looks like from this vantage point early in the twenty-first century.

Once again, you'll be invited to ask yourself this basic

question: "What skills and practices in listener-centered speaking will help me perform at my best to positively influence audiences?" I believe the answers—tested and tempered through centuries of theatrical performance—are in these pages.

Belmont, MA
July 2016

Maximize Your Natural Talents!

"Be brisk, be splendid, and be public."
—SAMUEL JOHNSON

How to Give a Speech will improve your skills in any speaking situation.

It will increase your confidence and charisma. It will improve others' opinions of your character and competence.

But it will do something even more valuable than these important things. *It will dramatically increase your influence with everyone you talk to—about anything.*

Any book that attempts such a task had better focus on your actions as a speaker. By that, I mean your physical behavior and vocal approach that together convey messages quite separate from the words you're using. These are the critical nonverbal components of public speaking, and they are the focus of this book.

How to Give a Speech, then, is a self-improvement book. It aims to substantially improve your public speaking *performance.*

Why should you worry about performance? Well, the answer to that is clear. To change people's lives in some positive way—to affect how they think, feel, or act as a result of your presentations—you must perform at the peak of your abilities.

Successful and influential speakers know all about reaching this pinnacle of achievement.

Think of the great orators whose names we honor, people like Pericles in ancient Greece, Winston Churchill, Abraham Lincoln, and

Martin Luther King, Jr. Each of them was famous and everyone knew what they stood for. But it was their stirring addresses in public, their moments of peak performance, that secured their places in history.

They consciously used their attributes as speakers to the fullest extent possible. They performed at their very best.

This book will show you how to maximize your own natural speaking talents in powerful and specific ways. The type of speech or presentation you give doesn't matter. In each case you have the same task: honest communication that reaches your listeners' hearts and minds, while conveying a clear sense of who you are and what you stand for.

Here, then, is solid hands-on advice delivered in what I hope is a compact and reader-friendly package. You can keep this book on your bookshelf if you like. But I urge you to slip it into your briefcase, purse, or carry-on and take it with you whenever you'll be speaking in public. It truly is a guidebook of dynamic public speaking, meant to be as practical as possible.

There are 101 entries in all, written as "Quick Tips" organized in sixteen chapters. You can read the book from cover to cover, or explore a topic that's on your mind at the moment, or head straight to any tip that catches your eye.

How to Give a Speech is the result of four decades of my work as a professional actor, public speaking professor, and speech coach to clients around the world. So it's filled with the practical matters these people have been engaged with as influential communicators.

I'd love to hear from you if you'd like to add to the contributions from this speaking community. Or feel free to simply give me feedback on the book. If there are topics that you'd like to see covered in future editions, I'd be delighted to hear about them.

Now a last word to you before your important speech or presentation. It's the traditional, lovingly intended advice from the world of the theater: *Break a leg!*

—GARY GENARD
gary@genardmethod.com

Calming Your Nerves and Gaining Confidence

"The mind is a wonderful thing. It starts working the minute you are born and never stops until you get up to speak in public."

—ROSCOE DRUMMOND

1: Got 5 Minutes? — Relax!

"Easy does it."

"Take it easy."

"Easy as pie."

In America, we admire people who not only do things expertly, but who make them seem easy.

I believe one of the reasons we feel this way, is that when things are going smoothly—when we're hitting on all cylinders—we're functioning at peak efficiency. And that just feels *right*.

Some people call this level of performance being in "flow," or nowadays, being in The Zone. Whatever name you attach to it, it's a feeling of effortlessness—an intense pleasure that comes from focusing completely on the task rather than the obstacles in our way.

The first rule of successful presentations then is to bring us to such a state of natural relaxation. Once we do that we can place our focus where it needs to be: on our message and listeners, rather than on the things that make us self-conscious and anxious.

But given today's hectic professional schedules, we also need a way to help us relax *quickly*. So here's a wonderful way to achieve a productive level of relaxation (yes, there is such a thing!) if you only have 5 minutes to spare:

1. **Find a quiet and solitary place.** (In a pinch, a bathroom stall will do, or even your parked car outside your speaking venue.) Sit comfortably, with your feet flat on the floor.

2. **Close your eyes.**

3. **"Listen" to your breath for the first minute.** That is, pay attention to what happens when you breathe in slowly and calmly. Understand with your body, not your mind, how breathing nourishes and sustains you. Feel the breath flowing down your throat, filling your lungs, and then bringing life-giving oxygen to every cell in your body.

4. **Now, focus your awareness on a visual image you "see" in your mind.** Make it a neutral color and shape: a green circle, a yellow square, a blue triangle. Any object that doesn't have emotional connotations for you is fine. (Avoid the color red, which is often associated with blood or anger.)

5. **See that object in as close to crystal clarity as you can manage.** This will take concentration and a bit of practice at first. As you do, adopt a passive attitude toward any other mental activity. Thoughts, imagery, and feelings will emerge in your consciousness. Simply notice them then let them go on their way. Keep a gentle yet firm focus on your image. Do nothing; just let your awareness be.

6. **Your breathing will become slower and deeper.** This is what you are aiming for. You're now in a calmer and more relaxed state. When you're ready, open your eyes and slowly stand. If you feel any lightheadedness, sit down again, for your body may not be used to taking in this level of oxygen. Once you

have it, try to maintain this level of calmness and *relaxed breathing* as you go on with your daily tasks.

This exercise allows you to calm yourself and focus your attention—two essential attributes of a good speech or presentation. Practice it until you can do it easily at a moment's notice, because that's when you will need it most!

2: Body Over Mind: The Progressive Relaxation Exercise

Here's another exercise concerned with relaxation. This time, you'll learn how to release muscular tension throughout your body so you can practice effortless diaphragmatic breathing. (For more on breathing and public speaking, see Chapter Two.)

Do this exercise while lying on a yoga mat or carpet. The first time you practice the sequence it may take up to twenty minutes to reach the state of relaxation described. With more practice, it might take you only ten minutes to achieve the same state of full mental and physical relaxation.

- Lie on your back, with eyes closed and arms and feet uncrossed at your sides.

- Follow your breath: Be aware of breathing in and out easily. "Watch" your breath as it enters your nose and goes down your throat. Stay with the nourishing breath as it passes into your lungs and then throughout your body. Feel how the oxygen nourishes every cell in your body. Become conscious of how refreshing and life affirming each miraculous breath is.

- Now, as you continue to breathe easily, focus your awareness on the top of your head. Be aware of a sense of complete relaxation: as you focus on that area, your scalp and the individual hairs on your head suddenly release all tension held within them. You feel a pleasantly heavy sensation like warm lava moving slowly down your head and scalp, gently melting away all tension as it moves.

- Allow that warm heavy feeling to spread from your scalp to your forehead. Feel the same release of tension, the melting-away, the sensation of smoothness and relaxation.

- Keeping the level of relaxation you've achieved in your scalp and forehead, let the lava flow down to your eyes. You may hold considerable tension behind your eyes—many people do. Let it melt away.

- Allow the warm melting-lava feeling to *slowly* proceed down your body. Each part of your body that it reaches immediately relaxes as the tension melts away. When you get to your fingers, allow any remaining tension to flow out your fingertips. And when you get to your feet, let the same thing happen through your toes. Don't DO anything; just let it happen.

- Once your body is completely relaxed, do a mental scan to locate any remaining pockets of tension. Then let that tension melt away until you're completely and utterly relaxed. Now, allow your muscles to "remember" what this feels like, i.e., register it in your muscle memory.

- Now that you're completely relaxed, and still lying down, place the palm of your dominant hand on your abdomen where it rises and falls with each breath. Breathe gently and deeply. Feel your hand moving up and down with the "bellows" action of free diaphragmatic breathing. *This is what natural breathing in a relaxed state feels like.*

3: Four Key Ingredients to Achieving Influence as a Speaker

The reason we give speeches and presentations, reports at meetings, sales talks, campaign speeches, and every other type of

6

performance, is to *influence* our listeners positively. Knowing that we have the ability to do so should give us confidence. In fact, it should make us eager to get up on our feet!

Below are what I consider to be the four actions on your part that are essential to achieving influence as a speaker. You should therefore include them in every one of your presentations:

1. **Establish Your Credibility.** You must have *credibility* in an audience's mind if you are to get listeners to think, feel, or do what you want them to as a result of your speech.

    "Why in the world should I listen to this person?" is the ever-present question in listeners' minds. It's up to you to supply the answer. And *fast:* during the first 60 seconds of your talk.

    Tell them why they should listen to you—and I mean literally tell them. What is your experience that allows you to speak on this topic? What's your job title? How long have you been working in this field (or pursuing it as an avocation)?

    Did you conduct research that you'll be discussing in this presentation? Unless you're already famous, you must begin to build your credibility from the very first word out of your mouth. Being credible is what makes you worth listening to and believing.

2. **Be Honest.** Does that sound obvious? Actually, when we lack confidence in ourselves as presenters, we usually try to be something other than who we really are. We wear a mask, or slip on invisible armor to protect us. Worst of all, we try to be "as good as" someone else who's a successful speaker.

    But none of these solutions ever works, because listeners only pay attention when a speaker is being completely honest with them. Each of us is absolutely unique in the universe, and therefore interesting! It is equally unproductive to try to hide from audiences, and to sound like someone we're not. To be influential as a speaker, then, show your listeners your true self.

3. **Connect with Your Audience.** Always remember that when

you speak you are there for the audience's benefit, not your own. So you need to find ways to put yourself in their shoes so you can understand and meet their needs.

If possible, greet some of your audience members before your presentation. When you speak, continually look your listeners in the eyes. Some presenters are so nervous that they look over the heads of audience members. But isn't it easier to convince other people than the back wall?

Equally important: watch your listeners' reactions. That way you can adjust what you're saying (for instance, to clarify a point if they seem confused or to address what looks like resistance to your message) so you'll always be connecting with them.

4. **Think in Terms of Action.** Most of us make a pair of mistakes when we give a presentation: (1) We tend to wrap our content around us like a safety blanket; and (2) We keep stepping out of our talking points to wonder (and wander) in our own minds about how we're doing as a presenter.

Although this is a natural reaction, it puts us 180 degrees from where we need to be situated in terms of influencing an audience. We should be paying attention to them, that is, rather than to our content or ourselves. After all, you should know your topic and who you are pretty well. When you're speaking, your objective has to be to get that material and yourself across to the audience!

I mentioned at the beginning of this Quick Tip that the reason we speak is always to influence our audience somehow. So again, think about what you want your audience to do as a result of your presentation. Exactly how do you plan to change people's lives positively?

Thinking that way will give your presentation real drive and relevance. It should also remind you of how much your speech really matters.

Now, go influence.

4: How to Establish Rapport with Your Audience

The first 60 seconds of any presentation is a killer, isn't it?

You're nervous. The audience doesn't know what to expect. And everyone—on a bad day, *you* included—is preoccupied with whatever is going on in his or her life up to the point when you started speaking.

So you'd better hurry up and deliver a strong introduction, right?

Actually no. That's the mistake too many speakers make. There's an important and necessary part of your presentation that should precede the introduction.

It's your *greeting*.

One reason a presenter and the audience feel awkward in one another's company is because the speaker hasn't taken time to establish rapport with his or her listeners. That only stands to reason: before you can begin to talk about your topic, you have to acknowledge the people you'll be talking to!

Your greeting is the place where you establish rapport, so it can't be left out. This is the moment you introduce *yourself* to your listeners, and vice versa. The fact that you do it verbally and your listeners do it through nonverbal communication doesn't matter at all.

Here are 5 steps you should take to gain audience rapport through an accomplished greeting. Doing these five things will help you not only start out smoothly, but get listeners on your side immediately:

1. **Look at your audience as you prepare to speak.** Whether you're walking to the lectern or front of the room, or sitting at a conference table, allow a moment for the relationship between you and your listeners to emerge. There's nothing complicated here. Just remember the playwright and actor Noel Coward's

advice to young actors—to simply remember their lines and not bump into the furniture.

2. **Smile.** It's surprising how many people don't smile when they speak in public. Why subject your audience to the grim countenance which often appears when presenters "talk seriously" about business? Even a eulogy doesn't require a look of doom! If smiling seems like a difficult task for you, at least assume a pleasant and open expression. (Incidentally, I suggest you smile when you're on the phone as well. Listeners will hear the smile in your voice.)

3. **Greet your listeners.** Feel free to say, "Good morning," "Hello, everyone," or "Whoa! Did you see that tornado that just blew down the street?" or anything else that fits the situation. In conference calls especially, a greeting is often left out.

4. **Gather your power as a speaker.** When you reach your spot, look at the audience silently for five to ten seconds before speaking. Allow the anticipation and interest to build. (You'll also make sure everyone quiets down.)

5. **Introduce yourself using your full name and title.** Your full name, not "Jeff" or "Betty," is part of your professional presentation of self. And your title is an essential part of your credibility. I even tell clients to *re-introduce* themselves if someone else has provided an introduction. You never know, for instance, how many people in the audience may have been chatting or checking their phone at that moment and didn't get your name and title. Tell them who you are and what you'll be speaking about today.

Now here's an important point:

Notice that up until now, you haven't looked at your notes once. Why would you? Presumably, you know your own name, your title, and what you'll be speaking about.

Too many speakers make the all-important moment of their

greeting a muddle because of nervousness. They look from the audience to their notes, to the audience, to the ceiling, etc., all while they're acknowledging the audience and giving their topic. Watch a number of speakers and you'll see it happening. In these situations, the speaker's notes often become a life preserver, and they cling to them so they don't have to look out at that large *audience of strangers*. But it's distracting in a major way and gives the speaker no opportunity to establish rapport with listeners.

Instead, you should spend this valuable time greeting your audience through your eyes, your words, and your actions. It's an early moment of your talk that packs a big payoff.

5: "What Should I Do with My Hands?"

If there's one question speech coaches are asked more than any other by people who are self-conscious about speaking in public, it's "What should I do with my *hands*?"

The answer is, not much.

Let me explain: People figuratively—and sometimes literally—tie themselves up like pretzels worrying about how they should stand, move, and gesture as a speaker.

I once watched a judge standing in front of an audience settle himself into an odd position with his shoulders, arms, and hands because, apparently, he'd acquired those body parts a few minutes before his speech and hadn't a clue what they were for.

During the 45 minutes that this distinguished jurist spoke, I didn't pay any attention to what he was saying. I was too busy staring, and wondering all sorts of things about how he viewed the world and what he really thought about speaking in public.

Obviously, if *your* audience has a similar reaction because of the way you hold yourself when you speak, your influence is not going to be what you'd been hoping for.

So why do so many of us leave our normal physical expression behind when we speak in front of others?

The reason, I think, has to do with *context*. We're usually quite comfortable with our physicality at work and in everyday situations with friends and family. But we suddenly become extremely self-conscious when we have to give a speech or presentation. Yet there's absolutely no reason why this should be the case!

What we should aim for instead as speakers is a kind of blissful ignorance where our bodies are concerned. In other words, we should forget about our hands, feet, and other appendages for a perfectly simple reason: audience members don't have the slightest interest in them.

For listeners as well as for us as presenters, it's all a question of *focus*. If you are utterly focused on your message and getting it across to listeners, that's all you'll have time for. There will be no bandwidth left in your mind to stand outside yourself and contemplate your hands, your hips, or your hairline.

If you're into the flow of your talking points, *your gestures will naturally support what you're saying.*

And it's exactly the same for the audience. When the engine of your speech is running smoothly, your listeners will hear that hum, and they'll be willing passengers on the trip. (Of course, repetitive gestures or an odd stance will pull their attention away from your message, just as happened with me when I was—or wasn't—listening to the judge.)

Your most natural body stance: Believe it or not, the most natural position for a speaker from an audience's perspective is with one's arms hanging down at the sides. I call this the "neutral position." From there, the arms and hands should be brought into play when a gesture is absolutely needed. In other words—gesture when you positively can't avoid it any longer! That gesture will look necessary, organic, and appropriate.

Try it right now: Stand up, and let your arms hang neutrally at your sides. It may feel awkward at first, but if you look in a mirror you'll see that it looks perfectly natural from the audience's perspective. Now start to speak, and only bring your hands up to gesture when you need to physically reinforce what you're saying.

Therein lies a natural and supported hand movement.

So here's the general rule to remember about hands and gestures:

*Any movement that supports or amplifies what you say is okay, and any movement that detracts from your message is **not** okay.*

Keep this rule in mind, and you won't find yourself pulling your nose every third sentence, or making uplifting hand gestures that seem to be saying, "I need to throw up, but nothing's happening!"

Now, go forth and gesticulate comfortably and appropriately.

6: Create Your Own Command Performance

You have a speech or presentation coming up. Naturally, you've been thinking about it. The truth is you've been kind of *obsessing* about it, haven't you?

As the gears have been turning in your head, you've begun to imagine all kinds of things that might happen concerning your performance—some of them right out of a Stephen King novel.

But why do you beat yourself up like this? If you're going to spend time imagining scenarios for your upcoming presentation, why not make them positive scenarios? Otherwise, you run the risk of creating a self-fulfilling prophecy, with some of those bad things happening because you've already paved the way for them.

So create and internalize a positive outcome to your speech instead. One way to do this is by writing out what I call a "Command Performance Movie." This is simply a way for you to visualize a successful speech before the fact, so it's more likely to come true.

The Command Performance Movie isn't a real movie shot with a camcorder, but instead is a scenario-in-your-own-mind about the good and positive things that are going to occur at your appearance. It should be written out using pencil and paper, computer keyboard, tablet, or phone keypad.

Include in your one or two pages your pleasure about speaking at the occasion; the way you accomplish all of your objectives as you go through the speech; the fact that the audience is nodding and paying attention, etc. Also include comments about how everyone seems to perceive you just the way you want to be perceived personally and professionally. Be sure to put in the specific ways in which you feel positive about the experience. One of the aims of this exercise is to lay a firm emotional foundation of a positive speaking experience in your mind.

The amount of detail you include is entirely up to you. That and the specific items you mention are only limited by your (optimistic) imagination!

The following is a sample Command Performance Movie. Yours will be different, since it will be unique to your situation and goals. Wherever possible, make your imagined scenario as close to the actual details of the occasion as you can manage.

My Command Performance Movie

Today, I'm giving an address at the Mega-Movers of the Universe Convention. I'm dressed professionally and tastefully. The audience senses that I'm knowledgeable about this topic and they look genuinely interested in hearing my speech. They can see that I'm relaxed and confident, and clearly looking forward to giving my talk and sharing ideas with them.

After I'm introduced, I step to the lectern, smile, and nod at the audience. I take a slow relaxed breath, and begin my conversation with my listeners.

I speak clearly and knowledgably in an easy confident tone. My voice is lively and engaging. As I make eye contact with audience members, I see that they're paying attention and look interested. I stay focused on my message, which I know is coming through loud and clear. I know this material and I'm really enjoying getting it across!

When I finish, everyone smiles and applauds warmly. They've obviously enjoyed my speech. As I return to my seat I overhear someone say, "Now that was an interesting presentation!" I know that this has been a rewarding experience for them *and* me.

Breathing Techniques for Public Speaking

"Breath is the link between mind and body."

—DAN BRULÉ

7: Diaphragmatic Breathing: A Key Public Speaking Technique

Ready for a secret activity that will help you become a confident and dynamic speaker?

Breathe.

Yes, that's it. Of course it's obvious that you should breathe correctly for public speaking. Yet there are some differences between breathing for life or *vegetative breathing*, and breathing for speech or *active breathing*. For one thing, when speaking to an audience, you need more oxygen to project sound outward. You also need to lengthen your outward breath, since speech consists of controlled exhalation.

Equally important, you have to unlearn the habit of breathing shallowly. Speech requires you to learn to breathe diaphragmatically or "belly-breathe."

The diaphragm is a dome-shaped muscle that flattens out to give the lungs situated above it somewhere to go as they expand with air. That flattening effect pushes out your abdominal muscles located below the diaphragm—which is why your belly moves outward when you inhale.

Diaphragmatic breathing, then, is a bellows-like action. It allows your lungs to expand completely while giving you a full reservoir of air that you then exhale to activate your vocal folds. And that's what produces the sound we recognize as the voice. Obviously, then, you need a sufficient level of oxygen to produce strong and resonant speech.

How to breathe diaphragmatically: Stand at ease, placing your dominant hand on your belly, i.e., the place that goes in and out most noticeably when you breathe. That's your diaphragmatic area. Take relaxed, medium-deep breaths. Feel the bellows-like action going on down there? Easy!

This simple (and totally natural) method of breathing produces some amazing results. Below are six of them—and note that they go far beyond the simple production of sound. Breathing with the diaphragm helps strengthen your credibility, authority, and believability—three attributes you absolutely need to succeed in public speaking.

Six Benefits of Diaphragmatic Breathing

1. Slows your heart rate and calms you physically.
2. Provides oxygen to your brain.
3. Aids your stance and appearance, avoiding a "caved in" look.
4. Creates the sound of authority.
5. Supports your sound to the end of the sentence, where the important words usually come.
6. You appear confident and at ease (rather than gasping for breath).

In the order of those benefits given above, then, good diaphragmatic breathing will: (1) Reduce your nervousness, (2) keep you sharp and mentally present, (3) aid you in appearing prepared and professional, (4) make your arguments sound credible and persuasive, (5) "punch" the important words and phrases that drive your story, and (6) give you the appearance of a practiced speaker who's completely in control.

But don't take my word for it. Listen to one of the greatest poets in our language:

"And the heart must pause to breathe," wrote Lord Byron.

Indeed.

8: Are You Breathing Incorrectly? 3 Ways to Tell

Now that you know how to breathe diaphragmatically, you can take the next step to mindful public speaking through breathing. That involves learning how to control the breath.

Remember, it's exhaled air that excites the vocal folds in your larynx thereby producing vocalized speech. In other words, without breath voice itself isn't possible.

I was amazed to discover just how critical mindful breathing is to vocal production when I took Voice at the Webber Douglas Academy of Dramatic Art in London, where I completed my acting training. "Voice" was the title of the course, but for the first two weeks we didn't utter a sound.

We simply learned how to breathe.

It probably won't surprise you to learn that the same breathing techniques that help actors should be part of your public speaking arsenal. These practices will help you improve your own stage presence through how you look, how you sound, and the way you control your physical presence on stage.

But first, you need to check that you're breathing correctly. So let's look at three differences between everyday breathing and using the breath productively for professional-level speaking.

Difference #1: Active vs. Passive Breathing. As you already know, the type of breathing you use in daily living is called passive or vegetative breathing. As that label indicates, this type of breathing doesn't take much effort. Sitting at your desk, or using your voice so it carries three inches from your mouth to your phone aren't activities that demand much from your breathing mechanism.

Capacity is an issue that matters here, however. When your respiration cycle is this passive, you're apt to breathe shallowly taking in only a small amount of air. But public speaking requires your escaping breath to both activate your vocal folds and project your voice outward to an audience. That requires active breathing. *To improve your vocal quality, then, start by breathing more deeply.* Allow yourself a full reservoir of air with each breath, for that's what helps give your voice resonance and carrying power.

Difference #2: Where the Action Takes Place. To breathe beneficially for public speaking, you need to correctly use your breathing *mechanism*, i.e., the anatomical structures that exist to allow you to respire. This is where you may have developed bad habits as a speaker (many people do), and so work against yourself in breathing effortlessly and efficiently.

There are basically three ways to use the breathing mechanism, and only one of them is the correct method. If you raise the shoulders each time you inhale, that's called *clavicular breathing* (named after your clavicle or collarbone), and is just wasted energy. The same is true if you breathe *thoracically* (by overly expanding the thorax or chest area in "chest breathing").

As you already know, the third and correct method is diaphragmatic breathing, in which your diaphragm helps initiate maximum lung expansion. It's easy to know if you're breathing diaphragmatically because your belly—not your shoulders or your chest—should bulge outward on each inhalation and return to its starting position upon exhalation. If you're not breathing this way, you simply won't have the lungpower to sound like you mean business.

Difference #3: Controlling the Respiration Cycle. Your *control* of the breathing cycle is where you can make it all come together to be in charge of your speaking performance.

Why is that necessary? Well, did you know that in English the most important word usually comes at the end of a sentence? (Look at what I just wrote: "at the end of the sentence" is in fact the point I'm making with *that* sentence!) We all know that the most famous utterance in English is "To be or not to be, that is the question." Shakespeare didn't use some other arrangement that buries the central question of whether Hamlet should do away with himself.

When you breathe passively, your inhalation and exhalation are about equal, i.e., they have the same duration. With speaking, however, the situation is entirely different. Remember that exhaled air is the source of the produced voice. *So every time you express an idea, you're likely doing it on one breath.* Of course, I realize that some ideas take many sentences to be expressed, but I think you know what I'm getting at here: Each time you speak, you are controlling your exhalation since it is tied to the expression of your idea itself. So the more you can control your breath so you're able to *punch* that idea that comes at the end of your vocalization, the more reliably your listeners will grasp what you're saying!

If you're like some of my coaching clients who ask concerning an upcoming presentation: "When should I become aware of diaphragmatic action to control my breathing?" my answer to you as well is simple:

"Always."

Breathing for speech, that is, should be a full-time pursuit for you (though once you develop the habit of full diaphragmatic breathing, it won't need to be a conscious activity). Given all the benefits of correct breathing already given in this chapter, can you think of a better reason to be breathing effectively at every opportunity?

Actually, there are some more reasons to use good breathing techniques for public speaking that I haven't discussed yet. Keep reading!

9: The Amazing Power of Exhalation

Here's another great reason to practice mindful breathing: Controlled breathing can help reduce the tension and tightness you may experience as you're preparing to deliver a speech.

There's a simple yet highly efficient exercise that achieves this effect. I call it "Directed Breath." Here's how it's done:

Start out with the slow, controlled belly breathing you've already learned in this chapter. You should aim for 5 or 6 respiration cycles per minute. Inspiration + exhalation = one respiration cycle.

Once you're breathing slowly and deeply, scan your body for any signs of tightness or tension. Now, as you exhale, *direct the breath to that spot.* That is, imagine that you're exhaling *into* that place in your body. If you're tense in more than one place, concentrate on each location in turn. The technique works equally well if you're sitting or lying down.

Take a moment and try it now. Choose one place or area in your body for greater relaxation, even if you're not experiencing any particular tension.

I find that this technique is amazing for melting away my physical tension immediately.

As a speaker, it's certainly worth knowing that the breath alone can help untie your muscular knots. When you get adept at this technique, you may find that even the first breath has a noticeable effect.

Practice the Directed Breath as close as you can to your next appearance. It will help you become a more relaxed and flexible speaker!

10: Inspiration for Conquering Fear of Public Speaking

in.spi.ra.tion
1. a breathing in, as of air into the lungs; inhaling. 2. an inspiring or being inspired mentally or emotionally. 3. an inspiring influence;

any stimulus to creative thought or action (*Webster's New World Dictionary, Second College Edition*).

Surprised to hear that the first dictionary definition of "inspiration" has to do with *breathing*? Yet that's completely appropriate, since clear thinking as well as a strong speaking voice to deliver one's opinions both begin with getting oxygen where it's needed.

Among the benefits of learning how to be "inspired" in this way is one I haven't talked about yet: using the breath to reduce speech anxiety.

Calming the Storm: If you struggle with fear of public speaking, the first order of business is often quieting down the noise and inner chaos interfering with your comfort level and focus. Good breathing is not only ideal for getting you calm and concentrated— it's one of the few ways that you *can* reach that state.

Think about it for just a moment and you'll realize that a high level of anxiety while speaking is a bruising experience: you feel as though you've been beaten up mentally, and sometimes physically as well. Add to this a loss of sleep or concentration, constant worry, the physiological toll that serious performance anxiety takes, and the results of speaking fear can be profound. In addition, the extreme loss of control you suffer while speaking can make it seem as though an electrical storm were taking place inside your brain and body!

To become a confident and dynamic speaker, you have to get this emotional and physical disturbance under control. You need to enter the *eye of the storm* where things are calm and quiet. From this peaceful center, you can heal, rejuvenating yourself and "turning down the volume" as you begin to apply appropriate coping mechanisms.

The Willow Tree Visualization: Here's a visualization that may help make this clearer: Imagine a willow tree in the middle of a thunderstorm. High winds torture the slender branches of that tree, thrashing them violently, and the willow's wisp-like leaves make the movement all the more dramatic. That's what it can feel like when you lose control because of excessive nervousness and the inner chaos of extreme speech anxiety. But now visualize the *trunk* of the willow tree during the same storm: it's unmoving, stable, unaffected by anything except true hurricane-force winds.

As a first step to using the breath to reduce anxiety, I'd like you to imagine that your breath emanates from your core, just like that tree trunk in the storm. Your breathing is equally steadfast and unwavering—your breath is a source of calmness and stability.

So when all else seems to be out of control as your anxiety spikes in a speaking situation, remember that *your breathing is your center*. You must always come back to the BREATH, for that is where life itself and serenity exist.

Get to that place, and you'll be far more in control of the speaking event and your personal response to it. It's a reliable starting point for giving a successful, enjoyable, and memorable performance as a speaker.

Organizing Your Materials and Telling Your Story

"When it comes to storytelling, not taking risks is riskier than swinging for the fences."
—DAVID NEVINS

11: The Step You Must Take Before Deciding On Your Topic

The phone on your desk rings.

It's the Senior VP of Sales for the Trans-Pacific Region.

"Xavier," she says, "I want to congratulate you on the outcome of the Mega-Mega-Project. Fantastic job! In fact, I'd like you to come out to Los Angeles and talk to my team about it."

[Sound of loud bell only you can hear.]

Immediately, the thought bounces around the inside of your skull: *"WHAT AM I GOING TO TALK ABOUT?"*

Right?

It's a perfectly natural reaction. When we discover we have to give a presentation of any kind, our first reaction is to start working out the content: Topic, approach, format, stories and examples, handouts, PowerPoint slides, etc.

Unfortunately, that's not the most productive way to approach your challenge *at this point.*

Why?

Because one simple question intrudes: *How do you know what you should talk about before you understand what your listeners need to hear?*

In other words, when faced with the fact that you must give a talk or presentation, you must start with your audience, NOT the topic.

That's because there are certain critical points of information you need before you can go any further. They include the answers to three questions:

1. **Who** is this audience?

2. **Which** type of information or persuasion will they respond to best?

3. **What's** the best method of giving that to them?

Once you've answered these three questions, you'll be in a much better position to grasp exactly the kind of content you need to provide and how to deliver it. Otherwise, it's a case of the cart leading the horse. When you've resolved those broad questions, it's time to get more specific, as follows:

- Who is this audience in terms of demographics, culture, and politics, socioeconomic level, and so on? ("Culture" here can mean many things besides nationality or geographic origin. Examples include clubs or social groups, departments within a corporation, religious affiliation, and so on.)

- How much information does this audience already have? What do you need to give to them that someone else hasn't already provided?

- What are their expectations and preferences for this presentation? For example, military audiences probably expect to see some PowerPoint; and management teams are usually more attuned to a strategic vision than too many operational details, etc.

- Does the emotional climate of this gathering have some relevance to the presentation? Examples include recent layoffs at the company, or yesterday's announcement of hugely improved sales for the quarter just ended. Your audience may be strongly biased toward or against your message due solely to this factor.

- Who has spoken to this group in the past? What did they speak about, and how successful were they in their approach?

- What else can your liaison or contact tell you about this audience and the occasion?

By answering these questions, you'll be much better armed as you approach your engagement. You'll be able to put together content that will give these listeners something much closer to what they need to hear than delivering content you've compiled without considering your audience first. And what speaker could expect to do better than *that*?

12: Know Your Purpose and How to Accomplish It

Let's assume that you've followed the advice in Quick Tip #11 above. You now have a firm grasp of the make-up of your audience including their expectations and preferences.

Now you're ready to give some serious thought to what you'll try to bring about with these listeners—in other words, your *purpose* in giving this presentation.

"But," you say, "the purpose is obvious! I've been asked to speak about..."

And that's exactly the mistake many speakers make. They confuse purpose with topic. But the two are very different.

In fact, far too many presentations fail because the speaker has no clear idea of the purpose that the speech is intended to achieve.

Your purpose is what you want to accomplish in a speech. What you say about your topic is what helps you achieve that result. Purpose is always stated using an active infinitive verb: "to inform," "to persuade," "to motivate," "to entertain," "to reassure," "to inspire"... followed by the specifics of this audience and situation.

I might give a speech at a national sales conference, for instance, in which I state my purpose this way:

"To excite the sales force about changes in the product that they can share with our loyal customers."

Notice how this gives me as speaker a specific and active goal— to *excite* the sales force. In other words, I could talk about the recent improvements in our software in a number of ways. But if my purpose is to actually excite my salespeople about the new features that they can then share with our best customers that takes my talk in a different direction.

Importantly, that means that *I will bring in facts, evidence, stories, data, experiences, and any other content that will help me achieve my purpose.* My presentation will be entirely different from, say, a talk whose aim is to inform my audience about the changes in our software. Consider, for example, the difference in infinitive verbs in terms of the direction they give me: "inform" versus "excite" or "challenge".

Now for the next step. Let's assume that in terms of getting your presentation ready, you've done an audience analysis (Quick Tip #11), and decided on your purpose (Quick Tip #12). You're ready to discover four methods of organizing your material in ways that will resonate with listeners.

13: Four Classic Formats for Organizing a Presentation

So, to review: your *purpose* is what you hope to accomplish in your presentation; and your *content* is whatever you're going to say, show, or do to achieve that purpose. If you think in these terms, your content will always grow appropriately and organically out of your purpose.

But what about a theme that you can build your speech around, and a logical framework that will get you there? Theme-based speeches and presentations are inherently powerful and persuasive. And when they proceed logically, listeners can stay with you every step of the way.

Here are four classic formats for organizing your speeches that provide structure and direction. Which of them you use depends on the nature of your audience, your purpose with those listeners, and your content. Any one of those variables can change depending upon the speaking situation, and your chosen format should also change accordingly.

1. **Chronological.** Perhaps your presentation lends itself to a chronological approach. A talk to employees on handling a change in company practices, for instance, might first take a look backward at the firm's history. Talks on historical subjects also lend themselves to this format.

2. **Problem-Solution.** Do your listeners need to be educated about a problem before you and they can discuss possible solutions? A problem-solution format would work well in that situation. If your audience needs a more in-depth examination, you might choose a Problem-Cause-Solutions style of organization.

3. **Comparing Solutions.** If, on the other hand, your audience is already acquainted with the issues, you may elect to skip the discussion of the problem and its causes and go right to possible solutions. Now you can discuss the advantages and disadvantages of each approach instead of giving your listeners information they already have.

A speech on urban gang violence, for example, might benefit from a Problem-Cause-Solution format when given by a nonprofit to the charitable giving officers of a corporation. A group of social workers that deals with gang violence every day, on the other hand, might appreciate a more direct approach that compares solutions from the start.

4. **Story.** Everyone loves a story. Can you frame your talk around a compelling story? We all have stories to tell—companies and organizations no less than individuals. If you frame your message in the context of a compelling story, with all the drama, conflict, and emotions that people bring to their actions you will have a very captive audience.

14: Using an Outline Can Help You Think

Let's talk outlines.

An outline, as your high school teacher used to tell you, is a superb tool for organizing your thoughts into a logical structure. But outlines needn't look like the classical form of "I" followed by "A" followed by "1." "(a)" and so on.

At its best and simplest, an outline is merely a framework to help you get down your main points along with evidence to support those points. How basic or complex your outline becomes depends entirely upon your own comfort zone.

If outlining intimidates you, maybe this way of proceeding will help: think of the process as merely jotting down notes or getting your ideas on paper or your computer screen.

For public speaking purposes, two types of outline are most helpful: the preparation outline and the speaking outline. (I am indebted to Stephen E. Lucas and his book *The Art of Public Speaking* for this dichotomy.) And yes, the use of each is as straightforward as it sounds. Let's look at the features and advantages of the two forms:

Preparation Outline: This is the outline you construct early in your preparation stage. It helps you corral your thoughts and place them in an order that makes sense. Worthwhile features of the preparation outline include the following points:

- Using full sentences helps you gather your thoughts.
- The logical framework of your presentation becomes much clearer.
- You don't have to write out your entire speech.
- Sections of your content are easy to move around and reorder.

Speaking Outline: When it comes time to deliver your presentation, however, you need a more concise delivery tool. Otherwise, your listeners will end up staring at the top of your head as you read the lengthy manuscript in front of you. Instead, you should include only key words and phrases in your "script."

Your speaking outline, then, should be much shorter than your preparation outline. It's really just a skeleton compared to the fleshed-out body of a preparation outline. The speaking outline is helpful in at least three ways:

- It forces you to look at your audience, not your notes.
- It provides a springboard to your stories and personal anecdotes.
- It allows for personal notes, e.g., "Remember eye contact," "Read list slowly," etc.

When you use an outline like this made up only of key words and phrases, you'll be speaking in a style that maximizes a connection with your listeners. Your full-sentence preparation outline helped you work out your ideas in complete thoughts, and your speaking outline helps you express them naturally.

15: Dynamic Presenters Tell Stories. Do You?

I'll never forget how I learned one of life's great lessons: Seize every opportunity that comes your way to get an education. Or to say it another way: Don't be stupid enough to let educational opportunities go by so that you stay stupid.

Here's how my learning experience took place:

I was in high school. Well, not that day. My friend Ron and I had decided to accompany a guy named Wild Willie from our hometown south of Boston to Hartford, Connecticut.

Wild Willie was a high-school dropout who was crazy about cars and spent every cent he had on wrecks that he'd tinker around with and somehow get rolling again. On that particular day, Willie was applying for a job at the Pratt & Whitney aircraft engine manufacturing plant in Hartford. Naturally, this adventure promptly acquired two additional travelers.

The January day was bitterly cold, and not long after we set out on the three-hour drive, it began to snow. We reached Hartford without incident and Willie successfully completed his application. But the roads on the return journey were now snow-covered and treacherous.

Somewhere near the Connecticut-Massachusetts border, our car spun out of control, hit a guardrail on one side, then spun around and repeated the transaction on the *other* side. When we came to a halt, the car resembled an accordion, though miraculously no one was hurt. But we were suddenly without transportation, in another state in the midst of a blinding snowstorm, and without adequate clothing.

A Connecticut state trooper gave us a ride to the Massachusetts line and dropped us off at a restaurant plaza. (I'm not making this up.)

So there we were: stranded 100 miles from home, forced to use our (blue) thumbs to hitch a ride northward.

We managed to get a lift to the outskirts of Boston, where I phoned my dad. You can imagine his first question on getting this call from his son on a school day. I don't remember what he said on the drive to drop the other guys off and go home, but I recall it had something to do with staying in school and the value of an education.

As I say, that's a true story. Would it work as part of a speech to high-school students on the importance of staying in school? Probably.

Why? Because *nothing grabs an audience and keeps them engaged like a good story.* We see our lives as the story of our existence—a chronological tale of one person's time on earth. As such, we measure the phenomenon of time in a forward direction: one event follows the previous one, allowing the "story" to unfold. Stories give us a sense of control over our lives.

But stories play another crucial role for presenters: they show us at our very best. When we're actively involved in telling an interesting tale, we shine in terms of liveliness, commitment to our message, passion, and the sheer force of our personality.

So tell the story of your company, organization, product, or idea. Discuss the real needs of the people involved, and how those needs were met or remain unfulfilled. Speak of challenges faced and obstacles overcome; the hopes and steadfast commitment to a dream; the continuing desires of the people in the room; or anything else that puts human beings at the center of your message.

Dynamic presenters tell stories about the things that really matter. You should be one of them.

Creating Dynamic Introductions and Conclusions

"You never get a second chance to make a first impression."

—WILL ROGERS

16: How to Grab an Audience

Do you have key information that listeners should retain once your presentation is over?

If so, you should become acquainted with the concepts of *primacy* and *recency*. "Primacy" states that audiences retain best what they experience at the beginning of a speech. "Recency" says that they strongly retain what they experience last. In terms of public speaking, of course, this translates into your Introduction and Conclusion.

This Quick Tip discusses your opening gambit: your Introduction.

Here are three reasons why your Introduction needs to be engaging and interesting *immediately*:

1. Audiences make value judgments about you, your organization, and your message in the first 30-60 seconds. After that, you'll be able to change those impressions about as easily as you can change a hamster into a ham sandwich.

2. Your opening sets the entire tone of your presentation.

3. The first minute is when you introduce your message and tell the audience why they need to hear it.

So, some critical (and favorable) forms of awareness have to be created in the minds of your audience members. But it's not going to happen unless you can *grab your listeners' attention* strongly enough that they tune in and pay attention. Achieving this objective takes some thought and creativity on your part—but the payoff is huge in terms of an engaged and interested audience.

Primacy won't have much of a chance to operate, for instance, if you use the dreary, "Today, I'm going to talk about..." approach to your opening. (I call this the Today-I'm-Going-To-Talk-About Syndrome.) This is a dreadfully boring way to begin, and I invite you to remove it from your public speaking toolbox permanently. Instead, ask yourself how you can lead into your topic intriguingly.

The answer is, you should start out with a *grabber*—something that engages your audience immediately and piques their interest in what's about to follow.

Whatever you decide upon as your grabber, avoid what I call introducing your Introduction. That sounds like this: "I'd like to start out with a story..." or, "Before I begin, I'd like to ask you..." The truth is, you've already begun! And signaling what you're about to say before you say it waters down the potency of whatever follows. Begin with the grabber itself!

Here are a dozen rhetorical devices that can be used effectively as grabbers:

1. Story

2. Question (rhetorical or otherwise)

3. Quotation

4. Statistic

5. Startling statement

6. Personal anecdote

7. Humor

8. Expert opinion

9. "Imagine" (followed by your vision of the future)

10. Demonstration

11. Case study

12. Today's headline or top trending story online

But really, there are hundreds more possibilities; and you're only limited by the knowledge that your grabber must be appropriate for your topic and listeners. The best grabbers get an audience onboard immediately. And often, they contain an element of surprise that works against the expected standard (boring) opening. Coming up with one may require a bit of work. On the other hand, it should be fun to create an opening that you know will wow your audience!

To discover for yourself how effective a good grabber can be, try this experiment: Take a presentation you gave in the past and create a new opening, based on my advice above. Videotape yourself using your grabber. Now compare this opening with the one you used in your actual presentation. Which introduction to your speech was more effective?

17: Don't Be Afraid to Advertise Your Expertise

Do you know about the Amazonian tree frogs that are poisonous to predators?

"Ah," you may be saying to yourself: "Isn't it a tad late to get that message across while you're being eaten?"

The solution, my friend, is advertising.

Those particular tree frogs sport a vivid yellow-and-black or orange-and-black coloration—combinations that are instantly recognizable.

Hungry predators spot them and think: "Nope. Not *that* one!"

Why is this of importance to you as a speaker?

Let's assume for a moment that you read and followed the advice in the previous Quick Tip, on grabbing your audience's attention with your opener. Your next task is to reveal your topic and relate it to your audience. (This should be self-evident but evidently isn't, since audiences are sometimes left wondering five minutes into a presentation what the speech is all about.)

Now that you have your audience's interest, that is, and listeners are clear on what you're here to discuss, it's time to advertise your competence or expertise to talk on this subject.

The reason is because all audience members ask themselves the same question: "Why should I listen to this person speak on this topic? What particular knowledge or experience does he or she have?"

Your influence will depend to a considerable extent on whether that question is answered profitably in your case. To avoid any fatal resistance to you and your message, then, you must let your audience know that you do in fact have authority to speak on this topic.

You can mention your current position or title, educational background, years of experience, recognition you've received in this field, personal experiences—or even the fact that you have a long-standing passionate interest in this subject.

Simply make this part of your presentation brief and to the point (don't make it too long and don't let it sound like bragging), and find a way to fold it into the topic as it relates to this audience. There's often a fine line between establishing your credibility and sounding egotistical.

Another solution is to let the person introducing you establish your credentials by listing your degrees, accomplishments, awards, reputation, etc.

At any rate, don't let modesty make you neglect to establish your bona fides. Remember those tree frogs, and how it's better to be memorable than to disappear without a trace.

18: Getting Your Listeners to Retain Key Information

Here are some sobering findings. Together, they should remind you that you have to work hard as a presenter to get listeners to retain what you say:

- Audience members listen with a low level of efficiency. They need to be told things three times, since they distort 40-60 percent of what they hear. [1]

- Based on research by Michael Aun, an audience's retention is strongly tied to the use of visual aids. Following a speech given with no visual reinforcement, for instance, listeners retain only about 10 percent of information. If visuals such as slides, charts, props, etc., are used, retention rises to 60 percent. And if a handout is included, the amount of information retained leaps up to 85 percent. [2]

- Audiences are easily bogged down by too much information. The average listener can manage one or two key points well enough. But once you've introduced, say, five major thoughts, your listener is juggling no less than *120 different ways* of relating the different bits of information! [3]

The lesson you should take away from these findings is clear: Your best bet for getting listeners to retain information is to offer *one major idea supported by evidence.* You should state this theme more than once in one form or another, and include visual reinforcement.

Obviously, to make things easier on your audience, you should begin this process at the start of the presentation, and pay attention to it at the end of your speech as well. Remember Quick Tip #16

---

[1] Claudyne Wilder, *The Presentations Kit* (New York: John Wiley & Sons, 1994), vii.

[2] Jeff Slutsky and Michael Aun, *The Toastmasters International Guide to Successful Speaking* (Chicago: Dearborn Financial Publishing, 1997), 77.

[3] Stephen C. Rafe, *How to Be Prepared to Think on Your Feet* (New York: Harper Business, 1990), quoted in Lilly Walters, *Secrets of Successful Speakers* (New York: McGraw Hill, 1993), 59.

and the concepts of primacy and recency, i.e., audiences retain best what they hear at the opening and closing of your presentation.

Combine that knowledge with the advice in this tip about how audiences retain information. You'll then have the best chance to make a lasting impact on the hearts and mind of your listeners.

19: Bravo! Ending Dramatically and Memorably

I'll do my best to end this chapter the way I'm suggesting you end your presentations: with a strong Conclusion. I call concluding strongly having a *clincher;* and the clincher for this chapter on creating dynamic Introductions and Conclusions is about... ending dramatically and memorably!

Remember that primacy is the concept that audiences retain best that part of your message that they hear first—so you should have a grabber that hooks them right away. Recency says something very similar concerning the last thing you say. That's where the clincher comes in, since you use it at the opposite end of your speech from the grabber.

"Quit while you're ahead," and "Always leave 'em laughing," are two well-known sayings that embody the principle that you should end with a bang.

Now, think about the Conclusions to all the speeches and presentations you've listened to over the past year. How many of them were memorable? How many of these talks even *had* a conclusion?

A common public speaking failing is the lack of a memorable Conclusion that drives home the speaker's message. For audience members, this can feel like being on the receiving end of a shaggy dog story. Or to put it another way: a speech without a conclusion leaves listeners hungry for the last satisfying mouthful of your presentation's key ingredient.

Do you want to leave your audiences unsatisfied?

Just as you hooked your listeners' attention at the start of your speech with your grabber, you must ensure that your Conclusion is memorable and vividly refocuses your listeners on your core message.

As with your Introduction, a solid Conclusion requires some thought and creativity. But here's good news: you can use the very same list of a dozen rhetorical devices I mentioned in Quick Tip #16 to conclude your speech as well as open it. The idea is to be sufficiently dramatic, provocative, humorous, or otherwise memorable so that your message will stick in the minds of listeners.

A witticism from Oscar Wilde or Mark Twain, a quotation from Mother Teresa or Mahatma Gandhi, or any of the other devices mentioned or one you come up with yourself can do wonders. I also suggest looking outside your field of expertise to find a connection that's unexpected and therefore invigorating for your audience.

For as the great philosopher Yogi Berra reminded us: "It ain't over till it's over."

Delivering Your Messages Successfully

"It is feeling and force of imagination that makes us eloquent."

—QUINTILIAN

20: How to Inspire Your Listeners

If your message is important, your presentation has to be memorable.

It's as simple and as challenging as that.

Yet how many of us—whatever business or industry we're in—meet that essential requirement?

Instead, the truth is that *most speeches and presentations are exactly like all the others in that field.* In those situations, unfortunately, the audience is condemned to Presentation Purgatory—that zone of free-floating anxiety where PowerPoint is the preferred instrument of torture and time stretches on to the crack of doom.

Don't take your listeners there, my friends.

If you have an important message (and if you don't, why are you giving this presentation?), you must find a way to make your essential points stay with listeners.

Another way to say this is: For your ideas to stand out, you must stand out. Don't be afraid to make a splash, to be different! As a start, take a look at the five suggestions below. (And feel free to come up with your own approaches along these lines):

1. Think about how this topic has been dealt with in the past. Why did previous speakers handle it that way? What particular advantage or disadvantage did those approaches have? Can you go with something different instead?

2. Try "suspending your expertise" in your business or field of knowledge. Imagine that you're new to all of it, i.e., look at the problem from a neophyte's point of view. Issues, which were too close and familiar for you to see, may come sharply into focus for the first time.

3. Come up with some interactive exercises for listeners during your talk. To many audience members this will be a revolutionary concept. So, revolt!

4. How can you shake up your audience's notion that they can be passive observers? Make it clear that passivity will not be allowed during your presentations. Ask questions… and expect answers.

5. Consider every obstacle—technological, physical, or emotional—that usually comes between speaker and listeners in this type of talk. Lecterns, seating arrangements, and a failure to establish common ground are some of the usual suspects. What can you either eliminate or include for the first time to overcome these hindrances?

You certainly won't want to deploy all of these tactics in every one of your presentations. But once in a while, take a different route. Whatever happens, it should be an interesting journey for all concerned!

21: Four Powerful Tools for Persuasive Speeches

Would you agree that a successful persuasive speech might really make a difference in people's lives?

Now consider this important point: every speech or presentation is a persuasive activity.

Think about it. If you're trying to get listeners to accept your point of view—however you're going about it—you first have to persuade them that you're worth listening to. This is true no matter how dry or technical your material is, and it applies even to what we normally think of as "informative" speaking.

A common misconception, in fact, is that it's dangerous to bring E-M-O-T-I-O-N into a talk about serious stuff.

To which I say: N-O-N-S-E-N-S-E!

When human beings talk to other human beings, emotion is present and in operating mode. The emotional response required may be overt, as in a motivational seminar; or it may be subtle, as in a scientific symposium. But passion is still there—for isn't a passion for that topic the reason people are there listening to you? It's an emotional response if someone shares your commitment to a subject, a field of endeavor, or a mission.

So let's accept the proposition that we're always persuading when we give a presentation. The degree of persuasion and the subtlety or lack of it will differ; but the need to persuade remains.

Stephen Lucas, in his book *The Art of Public Speaking,* discusses four specific types of persuasive speaking. I've adapted that idea into what I call the C.U.R.E. Method of Persuasion. You can think of it as a way to "cure" an audience's resistance to the message you think they need to hear. The method involves the following four variables:

Credibility: You must establish your credibility early if you want listeners to accept that you're worth listening to and believing.

"Perceived credibility," in which you're recognized beforehand as an expert, can help enormously. But you still need to look for ways early in your speech to reference your expertise, experience, or sheer joy concerning speaking on this topic.

Using Evidence: Your opinion may be exquisitely considered and of the best pedigree. But as far as your audience is concerned, it's still just your opinion. What evidence can you show to back it up?

Statistics, reports, testimony, expert opinion, stories, personal anecdotes, visuals—and anything else you think is relevant—is what you need to bring into play. Pay particular attention to what *this* audience would find convincing, for audiences always differ from one another in obvious or subtle ways. Make your assertion, back it up with evidence then tell listeners the point you're trying to make. Don't assume they'll get it on their own.

Reasoning: Audiences accept arguments that they find logical and well reasoned. Your speech or presentation therefore needs a logical framework, so listeners can understand how you reached your conclusion.

If your reasoning is sound, your audience will be with you every step of the way. Even more important, they'll arrive at your culminating persuasive point at the same time you do. Wonderful!

And by all means, take the time to familiarize yourself with *fallacies,* or errors in reasoning. Advertising and politics are the ideal places to understand how a fallacy plays with and twists the truth. Avoid this easy but dishonorable path to persuasion.

Emotion: As I stated above, emotion is a critical component of persuasion. Too often people shy away from emotion in public speaking, for no good reason. Just because something represents "serious business," doesn't mean it should be talked about in dry, robotic (and non-human) ways. You should use ethical emotional arguments to convince listeners. Otherwise, you're leaving the human condition out of the equation. Incidentally, researchers into brain injury have found that even totally logical decisions can't take place in the absence of emotions!

How can you understand and employ emotions in your persuasive speaking? First, understand the mood or emotional climate in which your speech is taking place. There may be reasons, for instance, why this audience—the same one you've spoken to a dozen times in the past—may be experiencing a strong emotional reaction on this occasion or at this particular time.

Second, incorporate emotional language into your talk. People make decisions emotionally then justify those decisions rationally—and the more life-changing the decision to be made, the more this is true. So tap into your audience's instinctual reaction, the in-the-gut response. Often, that's the more fertile ground for seeding the argument that results in persuasion.

Finally, where emotion-based persuasion is concerned, remember that you are there to legitimately persuade rather than to manipulate. Keep that in mind, and your persuasive speaking will be both ethical and effective.

22: Under the Gun: How to Prepare a Speech in 15 Minutes

"Barstow!" your boss bellows as you pass his office. "Sonia just called. She's stuck in Patagonia—something about a melting glacier. You'll have to make the presentation this afternoon to the Finance Committee. Two o'clock. Don't be late!"

"But I haven't been working on that project," you plead. "I don't know the argument she's planning to make."

"Get off your knees, Barstow. You know she's making a recommendation that we fund the new factory expansion, don't you?… It's 1:40 now—you've got twenty minutes. Make it good!"

Twenty minutes?

Congratulations—you've just climbed into the Speech Pressure

Cooker. In fifteen minutes, at 1:55 p.m., you will emerge from the cooker, red-faced, and trot up to the company's Jumper's Memorial Rooftop Terrace and Conference Room, there to greet the Finance Committee.

15:00 minutes… 14 minutes and 59 seconds…

If you find yourself in a similar bind concerning putting together a speech quickly, don't despair. Assuming you have a reasonable knowledge of your topic, here's a quick-fix tool that can be a lifesaver. It will have you delivering a coherent, logical, and dynamic presentation in no time flat. Just follow these helpful steps:

- **Analyze your audience (2-4 minutes).** Who are they, and what do they *need* and *want* to hear? (One of these factors may be more important than the other in this particular situation.)

- **Decide on your central idea (5 minutes).** What one thing do you want them to take away from this presentation, i.e., your critical message? Make it concrete and memorable!

- **Choose *one* organizing format from the list below (6-8 minutes).** These are ready-made to serve your purpose efficiently and effectively.

    1. **Position-Evidence-Show-It-In-Action.** State your position then back it up with evidence (any type of evidence that's appropriate for this audience). Give at least one example of that evidence in action, i.e., show it working. Then restate your position strongly.

    2. **Chronological.** Tell your story in a past-present-and (perhaps)-future format. This simple structure can make things crystal clear and be highly effective with certain messages.

    3. **Problem-Solution.** This structure both informs and gives the impression of considered analysis. It follows a natural progression then provides a solution. Elegant!

    4. **Tell a Story.** This is your best "hook" for getting an

audience onboard right away. Stories not only get listeners to pay attention quickly. They also release your own expressiveness and ability to persuade without self-consciousness. Because you're emotionally involved, your audience will be too. You'll touch the minds and hearts of your listeners, and your message will come *alive*!

23: Presentation Strategy: Decide On a Direct or Indirect Approach

When it comes to delivering your central message, you have a fundamental choice to make. You can use either a *direct approach* in which you speed straight down the persuasion highway, or an *indirect approach,* which disarms resistant listeners before you drive your message home.

The **direct approach** is simple and efficient. Here, you state your idea then support or amplify it with evidence and examples. It's straightforward and uncomplicated. Where the correct conditions apply (I'll get to that in a moment), it's definitely the best method to use.

The **indirect approach**, on the other hand, takes a bit more thought and some careful planning. This method is more like a magic act, a sleight of hand, since it involves *building your argument* right in front of your audience's eyes. Though it's persuasion via a more winding path, it's absolutely the wiser choice in certain situations.

Now, let's look at the conditions that will inform your choice:

Use a DIRECT APPROACH when all or most of the following conditions are met:

- Your credibility with this audience is high.

- Your listeners are positively biased toward you.

- Your message is not a sensitive one.

- The action you require from the audience is easy for them.

Example: You're the VP of Training for a direct sales organization specializing in women's jewelry. Next month's presentation will be a speech to new hostesses on how to organize house parties. You'll be telling attendees how to succeed in the exciting and profitable world of direct jewelry sales.

An INDIRECT APPROACH is a good idea when the above situation is basically reversed. In these scenarios, most or all of these conditions apply:

- Your credibility with this audience is low.
- Your listeners are biased against you.
- Your message is a sensitive one.
- The action you require of your audience will be difficult for them.

In these situations, you must *establish common ground* with your audience before you start to build your argument. This strategy allows you to overcome initial resistance and gain a more fair-minded response to the case you're presenting.

Example: Your group advocates an override to the property tax limitation that will be voted on in the upcoming town meeting. The money is needed to renovate six of the town's aging elementary schools. You'll be speaking next week to a group of elderly citizens. You know that these folks are on fixed incomes and haven't had children attending elementary school for decades. The override question is sure to be a squeaker, and you need these people to vote with the "Yes" side.

You can see immediately how a careful approach that doesn't blurt out your controversial message right away can help you succeed with this audience. Instead, you might start out by talking about how everyone wants the best for "our town"—certainly including the children—and how you know this issue is a sensitive one, especially for retirees. After establishing common ground in this way, you can start building your case about why your side's plan is necessary to keep the town a special place to live. And that, of course, means for everyone—both those who have benefited from the excellent opportunities the town had to offer in the past, and those who need their own shot at those benefits in the future.

24: "Simplifying and Selling" Complex Concepts

Need a way to make a complex concept more graspable by your audience? If so, why not borrow a page from media appearance training?

That is, why not use a sound bite?

There isn't a reason in the world why sound bites can't be used in speeches and presentations as well as TV and radio appearances. They work with in-person listeners the same way they do with media audiences. Their effectiveness as a tool of public speaking depends upon four characteristics:

1. Sound bites use metaphorical language.

2. Sound bites make unexpected comparisons.

3. Sound bites provoke emotional responses.

4. Sound bites boil a complex concept down to a single vivid image.

That last point is the important one for this Quick Tip. Here's an example:

Democratic strategist Joe Trippi once said that when a politician picks up a phone with a reporter on the other end, he or she is putting a .357 magnum to their head.

Now *that's* an effective sound bite.

The analogy is crystal clear, and the comparison is an unexpected and therefore interesting one. It certainly produces an emotional reaction in the listener (in this case, fear). Likewise, "putting a .357 magnum to your head" is a single vivid image.

All four characteristics are present and are used well. Equally important, the comparison has "simplified and sold" a complex concept.

Republicans know how to use sound bites too. Here's Sen. Everett Dirksen (1896-1969) on Democratic President Lyndon Johnson's military policy in Vietnam: "All the piety of the administration will not put life into the bodies of the young men coming home in wooden boxes."

Here, the unexpected image of piety somehow re-vivifying dead young men is metaphorical language that packs a wallop of emotional power.

There's one more quality a sound bite must possess. It must achieve some form of elegance—though it may not include propriety or even good taste. In other words, it's possible to include all four of the above components and still come up with a strained image that falls flat because it's just plain clumsy.

Sen. Dick Durbin's (D-IL) response to the Medicare bill passed just before Thanksgiving in 2003 is an example of a sound bite with rubbery gums and no teeth. The senator opined: "The Republicans will give thanks for this bill, while the American people get stuffed."

Here, the comparison is strained, and the use of language is infelicitous and clunky. This sound bite wouldn't raise a nibble of anyone's attention.

When you have a complex idea to get across to an audience in a limited amount of time, then, remember the Sound Bite Rule:

Use a comparison that makes your idea come vividly alive in terms your listeners can understand.

"Arresting low-level drug users is like emptying the Atlantic Ocean one teaspoonful at a time." That fits the bill, doesn't it?

You may not achieve sound bite stardom. But you can come up with something that helps your audience understand a complex issue a little more readily.

25: Is Your Approach Stupid Enough?

Speech—the way *homo sapiens* understands the term—is the uniquely human communication tool. As far as we know, no other species has an instrument of expression that comes close for flexibility, subtly, levels of complexity, and impact on the world.

Animals communicate well enough in the sense of conveying chunks of raw information. An elaborately dancing bee directs other bees to a nectar-laden field of flowers. Whale calls travel across many miles of ocean in eerie and beautiful soundings. Bird songs differ not only according to species, but also by neighborhood according to the precise geographic location of an individual.

But these forms of communication are not the human vocalizations of speeches, talks, lectures, and presentations. We public speakers communicate in much more powerful and subtle ways. We do so not only to classify, differentiate, and warn as animals do but to persuade and influence listeners about highly specific issues.

We often make a common and significant error in our calculations, however: we think almost exclusively in terms of content. We constantly ask: "What is the information I want to get across to my audience?" But in a sense, our content is merely raw information, of the type that animals use. We need to go further by effectively using logic and language, i.e., linguistics. Together, those two tools set us apart as persuaders.

As I mentioned earlier in this chapter, your opinion has little worth unless you back it up with evidence. Similarly, an audience has a hard time being persuaded if it can't follow the logic of the argument offered. As a presenter, you must avoid attempts at persuasion that rest upon fallacies or errors in logic. And since many listeners won't share your commitment to your topic, your argument likewise can't rest upon a leap of faith.

A premise that leads irrefutably to a conclusion, on the other hand, represents a strong validation of the ideas you're presenting.

Like a lawyer in court, you must construct an airtight case leading to your ultimate goal of persuasion.

Along with logic, the linguistic side of your speech must be up to par. One way to get it there is to understand that spoken language is fundamentally different from the written word. To be effective, your presentation must live and breathe comfortably within its domain.

Spoken sentences should be shorter and simpler than written ones. Words should be concrete rather than abstract. Most often, you'll be better served by sturdy Anglo-Saxon words than Latin words: "chew" instead of "masticate," "think" over "cogitate."

Consider whether your language generally sounds muscular or flabby. Do you use vivid, action-oriented words? Have you built in examples and comparisons to make your points vivid and easy to grasp? Do you tell stories to make your points come alive? Finally, do you include emotional language that resonates on the right side of the brain, where both emotions and decision-making reside?

Your persuasiveness will soar if you deliver a logical argument employing powerful language. Remember the mantra that the late Sonny Bono asked himself before a speech, repeating what a wise politician once told him: "Is it stupid enough?" He wasn't commenting on the ignorance of his listeners. He was reminding himself to simplify his approach to be as accessible, persuasive, and influential as possible.

26: Silence Is Golden: How to Use Pauses Effectively

Did you ever consider what a powerful tool silence is in public speaking?

Using pauses and employing the power of silence is one way to raise your presentations from the mundane to the exceptional. You needn't take just my word for it. Neuroscience gives us some interesting evidence of this effect.

More about that in a moment.

But first, let's explore the necessity of this seemingly humble public speaking tool.

Four Important Reasons You Need to Employ Pauses

Speeches and presentations by nature usually include lots of information—data, if you will. You therefore need to help your audiences by providing them with "stopping places" so your talk doesn't begin to feel like a long uninterrupted trek across dry terrain. Here are four ways pauses help accomplish that objective.

1. **To separate the main sections of your talk.** Listeners can only hold so much information in their thinking brain before they begin to experience an overload. A *significant* pause is therefore necessary between your intro and the body of your talk, between each main point, and between the body and the conclusion. Pauses at each of these places tell the audience, "Here comes something new," and in effect, allow them to press the refresh button in their brain.

2. **To let vital information sink in.** When you speak in public, you're usually at the mercy of the stress hormone adrenaline, which tends to speed up all of your responses—including speaking. Record yourself; and if you hear yourself flying through important information, remember that pauses at critical points will help your audience process what they're hearing.

3. **As transitions.** One of the places where speakers experience problems is creating natural and organic transitions in their presentations. Always bear in mind that although you know how the ideas in your talk lead logically one to the other, your audience doesn't. Pausing as you transition lets listeners understand how the last chunk of information you gave them is about to be linked to whatever is coming.

4. **To aid the working memory of your listeners.** Speaking of chunks of information, here's where brain research reinforces the importance of the pause. Researchers have found that speakers

who *don't* pause between phrases negatively affect listeners' comprehension![1] Our short-term working memory can only hold a few pieces of information at a time. Pausing is a vitally important way to keep your audience with you—engaged, informed, and enjoying the experience.

So tap into the power of the pause. It will help you convey essential information in ways that sets it apart in the minds of your listeners. Use this performance tool the same way actors do: to frame an important moment with silence!

27: In Trouble? Send an SOS!

As speakers, we all have to face a hard truth: There will be times when despite our best efforts, we know our presentation is sinking fast. That's exactly what happened to me a few years ago. I was conducting a workshop in listening skills for 50 judges of the Commonwealth of Massachusetts.

No pressure *there!*

In fact, it was the second time I had offered this workshop on behalf of a well-known judicial institute in Boston. The first time, I gave the seminar to twenty-five judges from a small division of the state's Trial Court. This time, however, there were not only twice as many jurists, but virtually every department was represented, from the Land Court to the Superior Court.

The difference in the dynamics of the two workshops was striking. Unfortunately, I had assumed that my audience of workshop attendees and the circumstances of the two meetings would be similar, but I was dead wrong.

---

[1] L.J. MacGregor, M. Corley, D.I. Donaldson, "Listening to the Sound of Silence: Disfluent Silent Pauses in Speech Have Consequences for Listeners," *Neuropsychologia*, Dec. 2010, 48(14):3982-92, epub Oct. 13, 2010. Cited in Andrew Newberg and Mark Robert Waldman, *Words Can Change Your Brain* (New York: Plume, 2012), 69.

The first workshop was held on the grounds of an exclusive prep school with a beautiful suburban campus. My seminar was scheduled for 9:00 a.m. on the first day of a two-day professional retreat. The participants were relaxed and eager to begin their series of professional workshops.

Virtually everything was different about the second meeting. This time, we gathered at a law school in a suburb 30-40 minutes from Boston by car (yes, that's *Boston traffic*). The time was 6:00 p.m. on a Wednesday evening. And believe me when I say that a few of those judges looked cooked.

But there we were, in a setting not unfamiliar to me. I worked for six years at two Boston law firms, so I'm comfortable in the legal environment.

I wasn't too comfortable that evening, though. For one thing, the circumstances of the workshop didn't appear to make these judges predisposed to listen with such a forgiving mind to someone who wasn't either a judge or a lawyer.

Even more difficult for me as trainer: these judges were clearly hoping to take away practical solutions for their very real on-the-job problems. Somehow, I realized early on, my pleasant experience at the first workshop didn't appear likely to repeat itself.

So I did what I advise you to do if you find yourself in a similar situation in which your knowledge doesn't match your audience's. I suggest opening up the issues to the audience members themselves to solve.

Here's how it all played out: Throughout the workshop, questions were raised concerning a judge's ability to listen more productively to which I didn't know the answers. But each time, I offered up that question or scenario to the group itself. I asked my own questions to re-frame the issue: "Who has experienced a situation similar to that one, and how did you resolve it?" Or, "What do you think of what Judge A here did—is that a productive way to respond to a lawyer who acts like that?"

In other words, I allowed my experienced and knowledgeable audience members to contribute information I did not possess.

Taking such an approach isn't copping out. As a speaker, you're expected to be an expert on your topic—which in my case was listening skills—not an omniscient and omnipotent being. Your audience can't expect you to have the answer to every question they ask (even while the questions may pile up in an alarming way).

Why not let the audience, in a situation like this get you out of a jam? When it comes to speaking to audiences whose experience is different from your own, remember this: The more specific the questions you are asked, the more likely it is that the audience itself has the answers. Why shouldn't you make use of this collective wisdom?

When my workshop was over, some of the participants came up to me to tell me how gratified they were to even be offered a workshop on this topic. I wasn't convinced of the success of the meeting; and in fact I was somewhat dissatisfied.

I felt that at times, I had turned into more of a facilitator than a trainer. But I knew it was better to do that, than to go down with the ship.

CHAPTER

Using PowerPoint and Other Media

"PowerPoint is a form of theater. It's a type of performance."

—DAVID BYRNE

28: How to Energize Your PowerPoint Presentations

When did so many speakers become experts at helping us get a good day's sleep?

PowerPoint, the presentation program developed by Dennis Austin and Thomas Rudkin as "Presenter," and named by Robert Gaskins, [1] is an application everybody uses and almost nobody loves. And no wonder! Too many speakers subject their audiences to a static visual device that's poorly integrated with their message, and about as engaging as counting the crumbs inside a toaster.

Every aspect of your speech or presentation is a performance—including PowerPoint. So how can you use this perfectly effective tool the way it should be used, not to induce comas but to wake people up to what you're trying to say?

Below are three performance-based approaches to do just that.

---

[1] http://en.wikipedia.org/wiki/Microsoft_PowerPoint

PowerPoint's Strength Is In Images Not Words

Ever notice how *literary* most PowerPoint presentations are?

You know how this often plays out: The speaker shows a slide with four, five, or seven bullet points then proceeds to read those points aloud. Why? Though it isn't PowerPoint's job to be the principal influencer in the room (my next point), presenters seem to expect it to deliver *everything*—from raw data to the reasons why that information matters.

But it's the speaker's task to provide those reasons. That's why as a presenter, you need to remember why you're using PowerPoint in the first place. PowerPoint is a *visual* tool not a literary one. Words written on a slide simply can't compare with arresting images.

So look for ways to pare down the language on your slides and replace it with imagery. Constantly ask yourself: "Is there an image I can use here to make this information come alive visually?"

PowerPoint Doesn't Persuade Audiences... You Do!

Even presenters who don't read their slides aloud often make a fatal error, depending upon PowerPoint to create the influence in the room. PowerPoint is a marvelous tool for displaying visual information that can't be conveyed otherwise. But it can only spit out what we program it to show.

The business of *why* we've included this particular information, or what the sequence of slides is meant to show, or how this deck fits into the larger strategic or thematic goals of this meeting—these factors maintain an orbit far outside PowerPoint's solar system.

So you should always ask yourself, "Do I need PowerPoint?" If the answer is yes, the next question should be, "How can I incorporate slides so I influence the audience the way I want to?" Depend upon PowerPoint to create that influence on its own, and you'll be left wondering why everyone is glassy-eyed, with itchy fingers and jittery feet.

The Art of Storytelling for Effective PowerPoint

Here is the most important "secret" of all where effective PowerPoint is concerned: Your story is what matters, and PowerPoint merely helps you tell it.

Visuals can help your message come alive; but they are rarely the whole story by themselves. In fact, the seductive power of visuals can make you forget that you're there to tell a story. Call it a "narrative" if you prefer. But the fact remains that whenever you speak to an audience, you're telling your story.

So use the following technique to enliven your slides and energize your audience: Focus first on the story you're trying to tell, then consciously decide when to bring in a slide that amplifies that point or idea. You'll find that often your slide should *follow* what you just said. Instead of using the "Click-Talk" method of inducing sleep via PowerPoint, you'll be creating interest and anticipation in what's about to come, e.g., "The next slide will show how dramatically our market share will increase if we're successful in this effort."

Who wouldn't be eager to see the slide that you're about to show?

29: The Four Golden Rules for Using PowerPoint

In the spirit of making every PowerPoint presentation a tool of enlightenment rather than an instrument of torture, here are Four Golden Rules for Using PowerPoint.

You'll notice that the rules detailed below spell G-I-V-E. In our obsession as presenters with delivering content, we often forget that we are "giving" a speech—in other words, a presentation is a gift to audiences. Similarly, the four rules below will help you "give" listeners a pleasant experience rather than "giving" them a nervous breakdown.

Rule #1: Give Your Audience Enough Time. Audiences become confused when a speaker shows a slide filled with words, charts, graphs, etc., then says something *while everyone is interpreting the information on the slide.* Audience members then have to ask themselves: "Do I read what's written on the slide or listen to what's being said?"

Remember, your job as presenter is to give *more* than the slide can, not simply to regurgitate what's up there. But what you really should be doing is amplifying or building on the information. To do that, you need to let the audience read what you're showing before you start talking about it.

Don't forget that they've never seen this slide before and need time to process it. Give them that time. Let them look over the slide before you speak. By reading the slide silently to yourself, you'll know exactly when you should start speaking. (If you're now thinking, "But there's too much information on my slides to pause that long," you've just uncovered the world's best reason to make your slides easy to absorb rather than impenetrable.)

Rule #2: Introduce Your Slides. This is a terrific way to create anticipation and interest in what's coming. And that means a much more engaged audience! Rather than simply clicking on a slide and then talking about it (what I call the "Click-Talk Method"), use transitions to link what you've just been talking about to what's coming up next. Obviously, your narrative—the story you're telling—is the enticement that keeps the audience interested in what's about to be shown. "What I'm about to show you next is the secret formula for how we'll quadruple our profit next year..." Wouldn't you be interested in seeing that?

Rule #3: Vary Your Pace. Audience members become anesthetized by an endless collection of slides flashing by regularly like billboards on a dark highway. There's actually no reason why you should be falling into such a predictable rhythm. All slides are not created equal. Some are instantly absorbable (especially those with a strong visual image) and can come and go quickly, while others need more time to be discussed fully.

Invest yourself in your critical slides and move more quickly through supporting slides. If possible, include other components in your talk besides PowerPoint to help break up the rate and tempo even more. Group activities, demonstrations, exercises, even a short survey are ways to achieve some variety. Which brings us to the final Rule:

Rule #4: Engage Your Audience. Find ways to step out of your PowerPoint and actively invite responses from listeners. This is especially important if your presentation is a long one. Ask a question, share a personal story, challenge or cajole your audience, hand out a visual aid, or include some other invitation to engagement. As your high school art teacher used to say, "You're only limited by your imagination."

30: The Best-Kept Secret of PowerPoint

The Cognitive Style of PowerPoint is a 2003 monograph by Edward R. Tufte, an expert in the visual display of information. It's a scathing indictment.

Tufte's criticisms of this ubiquitous presentation tool have mostly to do with the "low resolution" of PowerPoint, i.e., the small amount of information that can be included on an individual slide. According to Tufte, "PowerPoint allows speakers to pretend that they are giving a real talk, and audiences to pretend that they are listening." [2]

My own criticism of PowerPoint concerns the fact that it's a presentation device that's virtually guaranteed to lessen your influence as a speaker. Since you as presenter are (in Shakespeare's language) "the be-all and the end-all" concerning the delivery of your critical message, anything that actually reduces your influence is a truly catastrophic state of affairs.

Used as a simple tool of visual information, PowerPoint can be effective. Indeed, in some types of presentations—such as showcases for homes that are for sale or where complex diagrams need to be displayed—it is essential.

---

[2] Edward R. Tufte, *The Cognitive Style of PowerPoint* (Cheshire, CT: Graphics Press LLC, 2003), 23.

Problems arise, however, when presenters try to make Power-Point pack more persuasive firepower than it can handle. Power-Point is as effective and as limited in its narrow range as a pencil. I happen to love writing with wooden pencils; but a pencil in a speaker's hand has never convinced me of anything.

Far too often, speakers depend upon PowerPoint to make some lasting impression on an audience—as if the razzle-dazzle of a multimedia slide show can take the place of an intelligent and compelling argument. Such visual and auditory fireworks can never replace a dynamic speaker who commands attention and belief.

Yet there is hope for speakers who enjoy using Bill Gates's ubiquitous presentation software.

It concerns what I call *the best-kept secret of PowerPoint.*

The secret weapon in the war to make PowerPoint a dynamic presentation tool lies in the humble "B" button on your keyboard.

Here's how it works:

When you are in the "View" mode of PowerPoint, i.e., when your slides are being projected onto a screen, pressing the "B" button on the keyboard takes your image to black. Any screens on which your slides appear will suddenly go completely dark.

When this happens, I guarantee that every pair of eyes will look at you.

With your audience now paying attention to you instead of your PowerPoint slides, real engagement between you and listeners can take place. Once again an organic connection between you and the audience will exist—one of the precursors of true influence. Pressing the "B" button a second time will bring your presentation back into view at the same slide

I recommend that you go no more than 20 minutes in any presentation before you hit the "B" button and *re-engage your listeners.* Ask a question, introduce a group activity, invite a volunteer to help you with a demonstration, and so on.

Try any of these activities or others you come up with. But

use the "B" button to introduce yourself again to your audience. I think you'll enjoy the people that you'll meet.

31: Testing, Testing... Is This Thing *On*?

Microphones make speakers nervous, and for good reason. Something strange happens to our voices when we're miked. It's called *amplification*. When our words are suddenly booming in the air all around us, it's hard for us to judge the level of projection we should be using to reach listeners.

Mics also diminish our physical presence. To be effective communicators, we need our entire array of tools to be engaged: vocal strength and resonance, facial expressions, gestures, movement, and our relationship with the audience. With amplified sound, we sense that those elements have less importance. So we tend to dial back on the physical components that, since time immemorial, have made our efforts at communication immediate and impactful.

The challenge when you use a microphone, then, is to keep the essential interaction between you and listeners strong, even though you can't call on some of the tools you're accustomed to using to do so. Your primary relationship with your audience hasn't changed, even if the microphone tempts you to ignore the physical components of an effective speech performance.

All of this is to make this argument: You should ignore the microphone if it's necessary for you to use one, and give your presentation as if it wasn't there.

Don't worry about adequate volume, for instance. That's the job of the sound technician or whoever's handling that task. There's no need for you to lean into a mic as so many speakers do. Speak at your normal volume; and naturally, don't step away from the thing so your voice disappears.

A microphone is only there to make what you're saying intelligible. Achieving the level of influence you want means being your true and honest self. In particular, it means giving the type of presentation you're comfortable with, and not changing anything because of one piece of technology.

Being a credible, trustworthy, and dynamic speaker is challenging enough. You don't need a microphone changing who you are on the way to that goal.

Twelve Easy Ways to Achieve Presence and Charisma

"Be here now."

—RAM DASS

32: How to Look and Sound Confident

Try this simple experiment: Stand and expel all the air from your lungs until they are completely empty. What did that action do to your posture?

You probably assumed a "caved in" appearance making you appear weak and irresolute. Now, slowly fill your lungs up to their full capacity... .

Did that straighten you up? Do you feel more capable, prepared, and stronger? I bet you do—and I guarantee that's how your audience will perceive you.

You just used breathing, posture, and stance to change your level of credibility and authority with an audience. Amazing, isn't it?

Let's talk some more about how the use of space along with your management of time can affect listeners' perception of you as a public speaker.

Space. The brief exercise above allows me to introduce the concept of *controlling space*. As I said earlier in this book, most of us become wrapped up in both our content and our nervousness when we speak in public. If we think about physical performance at all, it's to reflect how uncomfortable we are in front of all these people, and that we don't know what to do with our hands and arms.

Powerful speakers, however, go far beyond this elementary awareness of nonverbal communication. They understand how greatly physical presence in all of its facets affects credibility and believability.

Speakers who "command space" in this way, positively influence listeners' responses to them and their message. The more comfortable such speakers appear to be as they stand and move, the more likely audience members will identify with them. Conversely, of course, awkward speakers just make us feel awkward as well.
And when we're that uncomfortable with a speaker, we tend to resist their messages as well.

Good speakers, on the other hand, reach their level of comfort by occupying an appropriate amount of space. They strike a balance between diminishing their authority by reducing their footprint, and gesticulating too broadly or pacing back and forth like a caged animal (or what I call "the motivational speaker syndrome").

You can experiment with what it feels like to stand without moving, as though you're stuck behind a podium, versus move powerfully as a presenter. Pay attention to the sensations that you experience (and what you sound like) when you're doing something familiar and enjoyable then bring some of that body awareness to your public speaking persona.

If you commit those physical sensations to your muscle-memory, they will begin to emerge when you're in front of an audience without your having to think about them. You truly will begin to look and even sound more confident.

Time. Just as you need to control how you occupy space, you must keep a firm grasp on time as an element in your presentations. On the most basic level, this means keeping to your agenda so you don't lop off important parts of your talk because you're up against the clock.

I once coached a partner and a vice president of a consulting company who were giving a presentation together, then attended the conference the pair was speaking at. The partner, who spoke first, couldn't resist going down paths in answering questions that took him far afield from his topic. Suddenly, the time left for the VP to speak had evaporated almost completely—she now had five minutes to give her 15-minute presentation!

In your practice sessions, learn what 5 minutes, 20 minutes, and 40 minutes feel like when you speak. And keep in mind that time is always extremely subjective to a speaker—who is always emotionally involved and exposed in front of an audience—while remaining basically objective to listeners.

And learn how to pace your presentations through the use of pauses and silence. (See Quick Tip #26 earlier in this book for more on this topic.) You may think silence is an unnecessary intrusion into the stream of your speech, but just the opposite is true. Listeners need permission to take a "mental breath" now and then to let important information sink in.

Pacing your presentation through good time management helps keep audiences tuned in to what you're saying. It's also one of the best ways of demonstrating that you have the confidence to deliver your talk exactly the way you want to, unhurried and comfortably.

33: Tap Into Your Natural Talents

Let's face it: for audiences the message and the messenger are the same thing.

Take politics, for instance. Or a court trial… How many of us would want to be represented by a lawyer who seems to be wearing juror repellent?

What this means is that to a large extent, you are the message that your audience receives. So you'd better be aware of the impression you're broadcasting!

This Quick Tip and the three that follow discuss ways you can increase your influence on audiences. You can do that, first, by maximizing the connection between you and your message.

The first important point to be understood in this regard is that you are a natural performer. As sociologist Erving Goffman reminded us in his 1959 book *The Presentation of Self in Everyday Life*, each of us plays many roles in our daily lives, in effect giving a series of natural performances.

That is, we shape ourselves to meet the needs of the situation and people we're involved with at the moment. The "you" shopping at the supermarket, for instance, is different from the "you" on a first date, or the one explaining to that police officer why you didn't realize you were speeding and will certainly be more careful next time!

The knowledge that you naturally give a series of performances day in and day out should be a liberating thought for you with regard to public speaking. By acknowledging that a speech situation is simply one of the many "performances" you give every day of your life, you can more easily embrace each such opportunity instead of fearing it.

In other words: there really is nothing unusual or momentous about speaking in public. You're *always* giving some kind of performance in the presence of others. Public speaking just gives you the opportunity to do it with more impact and influence!

34: Show Audiences Your Goodwill

Do you give audiences the impression that you're speaking for their benefit not your own?

That's what "goodwill" means for you as a presenter, and it's a quality that's absolutely essential for speaking success.

Yet how often have you seen speakers who seem to love to listen to themselves talk? For instance, the next time you attend a meeting or presentation, pay attention to whether the speaker is making an effort to be sure his or her audience is receiving the information being given, i.e., displaying attentiveness through their body language.

Does this speaker make eye contact? Does he or she seem to be paying attention to the nonverbal communication coming back from the audience? Throughout the presentation, does the speaker ask the listeners questions?

Just eye contact can make an enormous difference. How can anyone even pretend to be concerned with the needs of an audience if the notes on the lectern are more important than the people in the seats?

It just makes sense: audiences who think a speaker cares about them are infinitely more inclined to trust and be influenced by that presenter. Remember, you should be in complete control as a speaker. *You* have the power to shape the thoughts and opinions of others; and in some cases, to change people's lives.

To be a responsible speaker is to use that power benignly and constructively. Playing power politics with your audiences can reap short-term benefits; yet eventually, the message of whom you really are will emerge.

As a speaker, you must place your listeners front-and-center at all times. *Look* at people when you talk to them, and use facial expressions—exactly the way you would with a friend sitting across from you at Starbucks.

And pay attention to people's reactions. If they appear confused or uninterested, you may have to repeat a key item, state something a different way, or think up a metaphor to illustrate your point.

These are the hallmarks of a presenter for whom the audience is the most important presence in the room. Truly, "it's not about you," however earnestly you want to give a good performance.

Here's a touchstone for gauging your goodwill as a speaker: If you are fully and completely engaged with the needs of your listeners, you won't experience a single "How am I doing?" moment. You'll simply have more important things on your agenda.

35: Reveal Your True Self

One of the fascinating things about speaking in public is that it reveals so much about who we are as human beings. As I tell my clients and trainees: even as an actor, I would have to work ferociously hard to hide my true nature when I talk to people about something that really matters to me.

And if I did, all of my focus and concentration would be directed inward instead of where it needs to be: on keeping my audience actively engaged with my important message.

Accepting this level of self-exposure becomes difficult, however, when we perceive a speaking situation as something "different" and intimidating. That's when we become nervous and afraid; and in response, we slip on our presentation mask or don our invisible protective armor.

In other words, we temporarily become someone we really aren't.

And audiences sense it immediately.

We need to throw away the mask, to let our true selves come through for our own sake and the sake of our listeners.

We need, in other words, to remain vulnerable.

You may think that's too hard a task to accomplish in front of colleagues or complete strangers. But believe me, the opposite is true. Being honest with an audience makes everything easier on both sides.

Hiding from who you really are is much harder work for you *and* your audience.

36: Have a Dialogue with Listeners

A speech or presentation can easily seem like a one-way street: You send, the audience receives, and that's it.

Yet that's not how a good presentation works. In a dynamic talk or speech, information passes back and forth continuously. It's true that most of the information is verbal on your part and nonverbal on the part of your audience (except in question-and-answer sessions). Still, every presentation involves give-and-take of information and sensory input. In that sense, every good speech is more dialogue than monologue. So it stands to reason that you need to pay attention to the nonverbal communication that's coming your way as your audience's "speech."

That way, you remain flexible and *conversational* with listeners. And people are most persuaded when someone is talking to them rather than at them.

At this point you might ask: "How can I possibly converse with an audience that's sitting out there in silence?" Like so many aspects of public speaking, it just takes practice. Here's a good way to achieve a conversational dynamic in your speech:

In your next conversation with someone on a topic that really interests you, pay attention to how you express yourself vocally and physically. Hear how lively and animated your voice becomes? Notice how you move and use gestures and facial expressions? What about the way your volume, pitch, tone, and vocal quality change as you speak about your thoughts and feelings on this topic?

Now, consciously bring those aspects of your communication style into your practice sessions as a speaker or presenter. You may feel awkward at first, because you'll be intentionally transferring speaking behavior from one situation to another. But don't worry about that. You're simply teaching yourself to be more like your natural speaking self, not less.

Next, ask a friend to sit in as a practice audience. Ask him or her to tell you whenever you don't sound like the real you.

In this way, with each session you'll nudge your presentation persona closer to your natural conversational style rather than an assumed style.

And the real you is the one that's unique and interesting for audiences.

37: How to Get an Audience to Trust You

We have to be credible when we give presentations professionally—that's a given. And being credible means acting businesslike and hardheaded, with a cut-to-the-chase style that banishes all emotion, right?

Rubbish!

When was the last time you made a critical decision about your life based solely on reason, leaving emotion out of it? Chances are you've never done that. As human beings, we make life-changing decisions emotionally—from the gut. Only afterwards do we justify our choices with rational arguments, convincing ourselves that we were wise to choose the path we did.

There are important biological reasons why we act this way. You've heard about the "left brain/right brain" dichotomy, haven't you? The left side of the brain is the seat of logic, language, and reasoning. In the right hemisphere reside spatial awareness, creativity, emotions, and decision-making.

Did you notice that decisions and emotions are located in the same part of the brain? Why, then, would it make any sense to remove all emotional input when we're trying to persuade an audience?

Remember: audience members want to be influenced by you; so most of your listeners will not be actively resistant to your message. But for true influence to occur, an audience must believe in your honesty and trustworthiness. And that, of course, is an emotional response.

All of this is to say, that listeners are making decisions about you as a presenter at the same time they're responding to your messages emotionally. So it makes no sense whatever to try to rid your presentations of emotion.

However professional you want to come across—whether you're discussing sales figures, a scientific hypothesis, policy issues, or any other topic—you need to include an emotional component so that you reach the hearts as well as the minds of your audience. People outside your field, for instance, may think that your material is dry as dust. But those who are listening to you if you're speaking in your industry usually share your passion for the topic.

A speech, any speech, is a presentation from a person to other human beings. And that means that emotions will be part of the mix.

So rid yourself of the belief, if you have it, that "feelings" is a dirty word where speeches and presentations are concerned. Find the emotional heart of what you're saying: the thing that gives your message life for you and your listeners.

Discover it and let it show. If nothing else, your passion will intrigue your audience and generate respect. And then, of course, you can add layers of interest by how engagingly you speak on the subject.

38: Do This to Make a Lasting Impression

What is it about a dynamic speaker that grabs our attention and compels our interest?

Well, for one thing, such speakers possess *authority*. We may or may not recognize them as experts before the occasion of their speech. But once they begin to talk, there's something about the way they stand and move, isn't there? Such speakers know how to hold themselves and command the space around them.

In a word, they exhibit confidence. And importantly, they do so in terms of their *physicality*.

I believe that most speakers are confident in their message. They strongly believe they have the knowledge and ability to get that message across. The issue with presenters who need a greater level of authority isn't knowledge or commitment, then. It's finding a way to "broadcast" that level of passion—to *externalize* what they're thinking and feeling. And conversely, to keep their nervousness from being visible.

That may sound like a daunting task, but it's really much easier than you might think.

Externalizing your deep commitment to a message and your interest in speaking on this topic really comes down to one thing: using nonverbal communication effectively. Audiences aren't mind readers. They can't intuit your expertise, your passion for the topic, or your concern that they understand your message. You have to show them these things. Remember, first impressions are lasting impressions. So it's critical to convince your listeners right away that they can relax, that they're in capable hands.

How can you do that?

Keep in mind, first of all, that "how you stand affects your standing with your audience." Evaluate your posture. And think about how you occupy space—do you "take" the space that's allotted to you as a speaker, or do you try to minimize your physical presence?

If posture (your "standing") is an issue for you, imagine that there's a piece of string tied to the top of your head that goes upward into infinity. Someone up there is tugging gently and steadily on the line, straightening you up in a slow continuous process. None of the "Ten-*shun!*" of a military snap to attention should be present here. Your posture should be upright but not stiff.

When it comes to movement, use gestures that are inclusive rather than exclusive, i.e., an open palm offered to a questioner rather than a pointed finger. Take a step in the direction of someone who speaks to you from the audience, or at least lean towards them.

And please, don't be afraid to come out from behind the lectern if you feel the need to do so. You are allowed to use the empty space on the stage or podium! (Incidentally, a *podium* is the platform you stand on when you speak; and a *lectern* is the structure you stand behind that holds your notes.)

Finally, remember that just as emotions produce physical responses, it works the other way as well: If you assume a confident and authoritative pose, you'll actually feel more credible and professional, and your audience will see the difference immediately.

39: What Is Your Body Saying? — Using Nonverbal Communication

Now that we've looked at the importance of holding yourself well and commanding space (Quick Tip #38), let's talk about how you can maximize your skills at nonverbal communication. You've probably heard that term many times, and perhaps you've wondered what it refers to with regard to presentation skills.

Nonverbal communication means everything you communicate to your audience through your performance apart from the words you say. Your content (words) is a critical part of your message, of course. But studies have shown *that what you look and sound like* as you're delivering information plays a central role in the message that's actually received by your listeners.

In research conducted at U.C.L.A. and published in 1981, communications expert Albert Mehrabian found that *93 percent* of message reception comes from nonverbal communication over verbal content. Mehrabian was specifically focused on messages with a high emotional content; and speech experts have disputed the relative importance of his claim—and even its validity—ever since. But this fact is indisputable whatever the exact percentages: a huge proportion of your effectiveness as a speaker depends upon your appearance, movement, and vocal expressiveness.

A classic example of this dynamic in action is the opening debate in the Kennedy-Nixon presidential contest of 1960—the first televised presidential debate in history. Nixon at that point in the campaign was ahead in the polls. But how he *appeared* on television in that critically important initial debate hurt his candidacy considerably.

Viewers had no idea that the Vice President actually had the flu that day. What they saw was a man with a hastily applied make-up job who was sweating profusely in the harsh studio lights, and generally looking ill at ease in the new medium of television.

Across from Nixon was the tanned athletic-looking Jack Kennedy, who not only gave the impression of youthful vigor, but also intuitively seemed to understand how to use the cameras to advantage.

You're probably not running for office, but what your body and vocal instrument are telling audiences is no less vital to your success. Unfortunately, there's no magic pill I can give you to make you a more effective nonverbal communicator. But I can offer what I think is a valuable suggestion:

Spend less time on the *content* of your presentation, and more time on perfecting your *performance* in front of an audience: how you hold yourself, move, and sound. Some excellent tools in this pursuit are a) a mirror, b) friends and colleagues, and most important, c) a video camera.

With their help, you'll begin to see and hear yourself as others do. That's a crucial step in knowing how to marshal nonverbal communication to your success and profit.

40: Speaking with Credibility and Authority

Let's face it: there are times when you want to come across as warm and friendly in your presentations, a team player. Then there are other occasions when you need to project a bedrock image of absolute credibility and authority.

Achieving that second goal—a high level of perceived professionalism—is what I'd like to discuss in this tip.

If you're senior enough or your reputation precedes you, attaining that degree of credibility is usually easy. But what about these common situations:

- You're young (or you sound that way).
- You're speaking to listeners who are more senior than you.
- You're the first representative of your company, organization, or government these listeners have ever seen.

In these circumstances and similar situations, you're apt to lack confidence in the role you've been assigned to play. And with good reason.

Fortunately, the world of the theater offers an easy and remarkably effective exercise to help you. This shouldn't be surprising, since actors face the biggest credibility challenge of all: convincing audiences that they're someone everyone knows they're not!

The exercise is to imagine you're a tree. (Aren't you glad you paid good money for this book?)

Seriously, the reason I want you to picture yourself as a tree, has to do with the very important concept of "grounding." Stage performers understand that much of their power in performance comes from the ground (or floor) they're standing on. In the earliest forms of Western theater in ancient Greece, that meant the earth itself, since stage performances took place outside. And if our planet itself doesn't possess the power to situate you in space, what does?

In the grounding exercise, you imagine that just like a 100-year-old oak or maple, you have roots that go deep and wide into the earth. Like that tree, you are firm, secure, and unshakeable as you stand tall and proud.

Now, what do you think an audience sees when they contemplate a well-grounded speaker? They see a figure of standing and substance: a strong and steadfast presenter. If someone happens to zap that speaker in Q & A, he or she will be strong enough to take the blast and still be standing when the smoke clears.

Speakers who lean on one hip or cross their ankles behind a lectern, on the other hand, have a hard time convincing audiences that they're a figure of authority. Try it yourself: Stand with your feet set solidly at armpit-width (a grounded stance), then with your legs crossed at the ankles. Which position makes you feel stronger and more professional?

When you plant yourself firmly in front of others, the response that's elicited in your own mind is that you feel confident and prepared. From that thought emerge *physical expressions* of your confidence. It's a self-regulating cycle that continually gives you what you might call "strength of character" as a speaker.

Combine this deep-rooted sense of presence with the diaphragmatic breathing I discussed in Quick Tip #7. Now you'll look and sound like a person of consequence—and credibility and authority will flow your way.

41: Three Tools for Becoming a More Powerful Speaker

It's a lot easier to make yourself a powerful speaker than you might imagine.

And power—in terms of the dynamism of your platform skills and your influence on audiences—matters greatly in the world of speeches and presentations.

You may be the world's foremost authority on your subject. Yet the inescapable fact concerning presentations is, that you will be measured as much on your *performance* as on your knowledge or expertise.

Political consultant (and now broadcast executive) Roger Ailes understood the juncture of self and message when he titled his 1988 public speaking book *You Are the Message.*

In plain terms, your audiences will equate your message with *you*. And that's a good thing. Otherwise, you could send out a blast email of your speech and no one would have to show up—including you.

So from today on, think in terms of the "speaking version" of you: a performance persona that's the essence of you talking in your subject area. That's the person your audiences will find interesting. In other words, it's not enough just to be whom you are when you present. You have to construct a performance version of yourself. That requires marrying your honesty and truthfulness about your message to some simple but powerful presentation skills.

Here are three areas of speech performance to keep in mind in this regard:

Competence. Advertise your competence in everything you say and do. When you trust yourself and what you are saying, your audience will trust you. That's the first step that allows them to invest you with presence and authority.

Every audience wants to feel that they're in good hands. Make it easy for listeners to relax and trust that you are such a speaker. All it takes to start is for you to trust *yourself*. You can start by simply not accepting any of the negative self-talk you may be in the habit of unloading on yourself concerning your skills and how an audience will respond to you. Trust that they are listening and are receptive to what you're saying!

Did you notice that I used the word "trust" five times in the above two paragraphs? This is not a subtle hint.

Rapport. Find a way to identify with your audience's values and experiences, and externalize the connection by talking about them. Most listeners resist speakers whose background or known views are noticeably different from their own. Whenever you can, show that you and your listeners share common ground. Remember that our experiences, motivations and feelings unite all of us around the world far more than they divide us. Create an atmosphere in your presentations that fosters persuasion and believability.

And remember to be interesting! You can judge this yourself in your practice sessions. If you're looking forward to just getting this painful experience over with, your audience will concur.

Delivery. Every audience arrives with preconceptions about a speaker. These may have nothing to do with you personally but are tied to the topic, organization, or viewpoint you represent.

You need to show that you are able to deliver on the implied promise that your presentation has created, i.e., that it will be worth spending time and effort to listen to. That's what *delivery* means in this respect. When you give your speech dynamically and with conviction, you'll be "delivering" the goods!

Credibility resides in speakers who appear confident and

committed. And of course, there's simply no substitute for enthusiasm. Embody your arguments with an energetic speaking style, and you'll go a long way toward changing the thinking and behavior of your audience.

42: Five Ways to Captivate Any Audience and Speak with Charisma

How comfortable are you in front of a public speaking audience? And what are you hoping to achieve?

If you're prepared to deliver information and get off stage, you'll probably achieve an average level of success. But if you want to captivate listeners, be memorable—and most important of all—move audiences to action…

Well, now you're talking!

So assuming you have something important to say and you're talking to an audience that needs to hear it, here are five performance-based techniques for speaking with charisma and impact.

1. **Make strong eye contact.** Simply put, no behavior is as fundamental to persuasion as looking at the person you're talking to. When was the last time you trusted someone who wouldn't look you in the eye?

    So actively look at and relate to your audience when you speak. When I say "actively," I mean let your gaze linger for a half-second to a second. Don't "flick" your eyes at your listeners. They'll like you more; they'll decide that you're honest; and most important they'll be more willing to be influenced by you. And ignore the silly advice from some speech coaches about looking at individuals for specific amounts of time or making eye contact with one person per sentence, etc.

2. **Have fun.** Now *there's* a novel concept in public speaking! Somehow, we've imbued speaking in public with an aura of

inconvenience, horror, and even torture—so much so that public speaking rates higher than death in lists of people's worst fears.

But think about your own experiences as an audience member. Are you more comfortable listening to a speaker who's grimly carrying on, or one who seems to be enjoying the experience?

When you speak with verve, you broadcast a completely different message than "I'm doing hard work here." Instead, your audience sees a person who not only has something valuable to say, but appreciates the opportunity to say it. "It must be good stuff," you can almost hear them thinking—"look at how much he or she likes talking about it!" Pretty soon, they're enjoying themselves as well.

3. **Smile.** As public speakers, we just don't smile enough. Smiling is a prerequisite to establishing trust with audiences, only slightly less important than eye contact. At the very least, it's evidence of the enjoyment I mentioned above.

In speaking situations where you feel a smile is inappropriate, simply "open" your countenance by assuming a more pleasant expression by raising your cheekbones. As an illustration of what I mean by this, look at the famous painting *American Gothic*—that's the one of the sour-looking farmer with the pitchfork standing next to his sister. Now compare it with the *Mona Lisa*. There's a lady who knew how to raise her cheekbones, and look at how successful she's been!

4. **Energize your voice.** Have you ever had to strain to hear a speaker? Soft-talkers and under-energized presenters make listeners do too much work. Worse, a speaker like that seems distant, and audiences feel somehow that they've been left out of the loop.

You need always to generate enough vocal power and energy to reach every listener in the room, including the people in the back and those that are hard of hearing. Remember also that your vocal energy must change in different spaces:

the larger the speaking venue, the more you must project your voice. (Obviously, you shouldn't increase your volume if you're wearing a microphone.) In spaces that echo, you'll have to speak more slowly so you don't override your own speech.

When you project sufficient energy in a presentation you make everything easier for your listeners. They feel they can relax instead of working overtime to do part of your job for you.

5. **Be aware of your nonverbal messages.** Visuals have tremendous power in public speaking—and the most important visual is you. What your body tells the audience is no less critical to your success than what your voice and the words are saying.

    Keep two factors in mind concerning nonverbals: (1) consider how you can give *physical expression* to what you're saying. And (2) make your words and gestures congruent, i.e., use body language that matches what you're saying. (An example of a non-congruent message: Shaking your head back and forth as you say, "Yes.")

    Practice in front of a mirror or video camera. Then forget about your gestures when you speak. Your focus and all your attention should be on your message and getting it across to your listeners—not on using a gesture because of its effect. If you've internalized the skills of body language, supportive gestures will be there for you without any calculated thought on your part.

43: Your Best Visual Aid Is... You!

Remember Bill Clinton?

Whether you favor Che Guevara T-shirts or quote William F. Buckley at cocktail parties—in other words, whatever your political persuasion—you'll probably agree with me that William Jefferson Clinton was and is a charismatic speaker.

What makes President Clinton so good at the lectern? Certainly, he's smooth. And he displays an extraordinary sense of ease, coupled with firm control. Not many speakers, after all, could deliver a nationally televised address from memory while a TelePrompTer relentlessly rolled out the wrong speech!

Perhaps Clinton's chief attribute as a speaker, however, is the pure enjoyment he displays speaking to audiences.

But let's step back a moment, and ask ourselves how we know that. How is it possible that we can reasonably guess Clinton's feelings about speaking in public since we're not mind readers?

Well, it's obvious *visually* isn't it? The body language; the easy stance and gestures; the frequent smiles; and the sheer joy of performing. All of these things declare that this is a man who lives for these moments in his professional life.

Bill Clinton, then, is an excellent example of an important phenomenon in public speaking, one that most speakers aren't aware of: *you yourself are always your best visual aid.*

Visuals in general are strongly seductive in public speaking. Charts, graphs, PowerPoint slides, handouts, video clips, and other visual aids are essential components of many or most of our presentations. But your most important visual persuader isn't any of these elements. It's you.

Think about it for a moment: You are the one visual component of your speech that's always on stage front and center. You are the visual that doesn't just sit there, but walks and talks and argues convincingly—the one that shares the beliefs of the audience and speaks to them from common ground. You're also the only visual that can adapt as need be, thinking on your feet and changing your presentation in response to audience input.

All very powerful stuff.

So don't relinquish your power as a visual persuader to your visual aids. Your audience has seen endless charts and PowerPoint slides and workbooks. But they have either never seen you, or they haven't seen you taking about this topic *today.*

Spend the time you think is necessary to put together the visual components of your presentation. Those elements are still excellent forms of evidence. Learn the techniques of working effectively with visuals, and practice going through your PowerPoint show.

But *before* you do all that, give some serious thought to how you'll look and move in front of your audience as you deliver your compelling arguments. The visual element of your speech that is "you," is a hugely important persuader. Find ways to make it work to your advantage.

The Power of Your Voice

"Invent the phrase at the very moment it is uttered."

—JOHN BARTON

44: The 5 Essential Vocal Tools

Let's assume that a Vocal Godmother has just offered you five magic tools that will keep your audiences attentive, engaged, and thoroughly informed and persuaded concerning your topic. Your voice, in other words, will now turn people on to what you're saying.

You agree on the spot, of course. As you sit eagerly awaiting your transformation, your vocal savior opens her magic toolbox. These are the five gifts she hands you, one by one—reminding you that they should be used together for greatest effect:

1. Emphasis and energy
2. Pitch inflection
3. Rhythm and pacing
4. Pauses and silence
5. Vocal quality

Now she explains each gift to you in turn:

"**Emphasis**," my dear [she says], "is simply the force or stress you place on important ideas, concepts, or feelings. It's the simplest of the tools, and I'm sure you already use it instinctively. If English is a second language for you, there may be places where the emphasis is slightly wrong, but that's probably all. Remember also, though, you need to speak with sufficient **energy** to engage the attention of listeners.

"**Pitch inflection.** As you probably already know, my pet, 'pitch' refers to where your voice is placed on the musical scale. Lively pitch inflection helps you avoid monotony and also convey meaning. It's a wonderful tool indeed!

"If you find, for instance, that your voice has a 'flat' quality without many variations in pitch, there's a good possibility that self-consciousness about speaking in public is inhibiting your expression.

"But you don't have this problem sitting around chatting with friends, do you? To strengthen your pitch inflection, find yourself a children's book, and read as if you're telling the story to a 3-year-old. That's when your voice assumes wide swings in pitch as you speak in pastels so your listener will understand. Tape yourself reading like this then listen.

"You see how flexible your vocal pitch can be? Now, having heard the result, you should feel more confident about using a more varied vocal pitch in your presentations… even to BIG people!"

"**Rhythm and pacing.** You mustn't ever be neglectful enough to let the rhythm and pace of your speech stay the same throughout. Instead, you need to vary things a bit.

"Variations in rhythm and pace aren't to be added artificially, however. They should emerge naturally from changes in the ideas, meaning, and emotions of what you're saying. If you're completely focused on your subject matter this will happen.

"Let me repeat: changes in rhythm should not be imposed on your presentation, as in 'I'll speak more slowly here, and this is where I'll speed up,' etc. Instead, give your full attention to your message and how it is being received, and you'll sound good as you speak it."

"**Using pauses and silence.** Here we have the most neglected of the essential vocal tools! Pauses will help you achieve impact, add emphasis, build suspense, bridge ideas, 'comment' on what you've said, and accomplish many other things that will help make sense of your text. Pauses also convey relaxation and confidence in a speaker.

"You should pause after an important word or phrase so it strengthens that idea in listeners' minds. Pauses also aid sense, since related ideas are naturally grouped together when you speak, and you instinctively pause when you're going on to something new."

"**Vocal quality** concerns the tone, richness, pleasantness, and emotional connection that you achieve through speaking. It's also an important factor in an audience's judgment of your motives and intentions, since human beings are highly skilled in perceiving the nuances in others' voices. Vocal quality is, in a way, the culmination of the other four tools.

"Use the five vocal tools wisely, and you'll simply be a more dynamic speaker. You'll also sound more connected with the audience, and sincerely interested in your topic and your listeners.

"Good luck, dear!"

And with that… she vanishes.

45: Developing a Warmer and More Pleasant Voice

As a speaker, it's your job to get critical information or viewpoints across to listeners, and to be audible doing it. Apart from that, why should you be concerned about the quality of your voice?

You should be very concerned, since your voice is the most flexible instrument you own for persuading and influencing others.

The human voice, in fact, is a supple agent of intention and subtlety of expression. Nothing else in your presentation toolbox equals it—not even the visual impression you convey. Where visual clues are absent (in phone calls, for instance), the voice reigns even more supreme.

As you've already seen in earlier parts of this book, the way you look and sound together bestows maximum credibility and believability concerning your intentions and your message.

Let's look at how you can fine-tune the marvelous instrument that makes possible the vocal part of your performance.

If your voice sounds harsh or otherwise counterproductive to your speaking goals, you should start at the most basic level of improvement, i.e., with the breath.

The best method for achieving fullness of sound in public speaking, in fact, involves diaphragmatic or belly breathing (see also Quick Tip #7, "Diaphragmatic Breathing: A Key Public Speaking Technique").

Breathing diaphragmatically not only produces sufficient energy for a strong vocal presence; it also provides a "cushion" of air that softens the voice. The combination results in a speaker who sounds calm, pleasant, and confident.

Shallow breathing, on the other hand, creates a voice that's thin and lightweight and can also give the impression that you're hurried. The average American speaks at a rate of 150-180 words per minute. If, however, you're racing along due to shallow breathing resulting in a "rushed" sound, you can easily exceed that range and make your listeners feel exhausted.

The second essential point regarding attaining a pleasant and warm voice has to do with anatomy. For, not surprisingly, your voice reflects what is going on in the rest of your body.

If you are frazzled and tense, your body reacts audibly as well as visibly. Just as we can see that someone is not calm and centered emotionally, for example, we can hear it in his or her voice.

Speaker A may be shuffling with her notes under the lectern, coming in and out of appropriate distance from the microphone, and allowing her breathing to reflect her disordered physical state. That in turn gives her voice a tinge of distance and distractedness.

Speaker B, on the other hand, is focused on her message and her listeners, and so demonstrates the quality of being fully present. Her voice is poised to respond to the needs of her listeners concerning her topic, and so she emerges as a solid, steady, and strong presenter.

Which speaker would you rather listen to? Which would you rather be?

46: Finding the Pitch that's Right For You

We often speak about the "pitch" of someone's voice. But what exactly does that mean?

As Quick Tip #44 above mentioned, pitch refers to the placement of the voice on the musical scale: its highness or lowness. A voice with an extremely low pitch, such as Henry Kissinger's, has a basso profundo quality to it. Comedian Pee Wee Herman's professional voice, on the other hands, seems as light and wind-blown as a feather.

As a speaking professional, you should know about two aspects of this important vocal tool: habitual pitch and optimal pitch. The vocal pitch you use out of habit, that is, may not be the one best suited for your physiology, vocal health, and pleasantness for listeners. Those characteristics reside in your "optimal pitch."

Males and females not only have differences in the size of their vocal structures; they also can develop opposite behaviors in terms of habitual vs. optimal pitch. Men have a tendency to sit on their pitch, forcing it down into their lowest registers where they believe they sound most masculine and authoritative. Women, however, sometimes head in the opposite direction, lightening their voices artificially to sound sweet and girlish.

You may not take either approach, and of course you shouldn't. But too many of us are guilty of using an undifferentiated pitch that gives our speech an uninflected and monotonous quality.

In any case, it's worth knowing whether the pitch you're using is right for you in terms of vocal health and quality of sound production. Here are two quick-and-easy ways to find out:

Method #1: Without thinking about it beforehand, record yourself singing "Happy Birthday." Now immediately say something into the tape recorder in what you consider your normal voice. The two recordings—the song and the spoken passage—should match fairly closely in terms of highness or lowness on the musical scale. If they don't, "Happy Birthday" is closer to your optimal pitch because it was spontaneous.

Method #2: Sing a sustained note somewhere in the middle of your vocal range. Now "step down" one note on the musical scale at a time, i.e., "Do," "Ti," "La," "So," and so on. Continue until you reach the lowest note you can sustain without the sound breaking up. Now, come up two or three notes on the scale. That's your optimal pitch.

If you've just found that your habitual pitch (the one you're accustomed to using) doesn't match your optimal pitch (your healthiest and most effective pitch), make any necessary adjustments. Now try using what you know is your optimal pitch regularly.

Don't be discouraged if it takes time for you to get used to your new pitch. You may have been using a not-so-good-for-you pitch for years. After all, that's one of the definitions of habit, isn't it? With time and a bit of concentration, though, you'll develop a new and more beneficial vocal habit.

You might say it's as easy as Do-Re-Me!

47: Are You Singing Your Speech or Just Mouthing the Words?

Did you ever consider that delivering an outstanding presentation is like performing a great song? Not only is the "music" delightful for your audience to listen to but your voice soars on a combination of dynamic technique and an inspirational message. The way you use your vocal tools, that is, carries astonishing weight with regard to credibility, authority, and that all-important attribute, believability.

Why does your voice alone make such a difference? Well, for one thing we all respond in basic and even primitive ways to the qualities of a person's voice. If a voice is pleasant and authoritative, for instance, it inspires confidence in the listener. But a voice that comes across as unpleasant, weak or too timid nudges that same listener in the opposite direction.

Vocal dynamics or vocal variety is one of the most powerful tools that presenters possess to win over audiences. The elements of vocal dynamics—tone quality, pitch placement, inflection, use of emphasis, variations in pace and tempo, employing pauses, and all the emotional nuances your voice can project—offer you a nearly limitless palette to "paint word pictures" and convince others. When you employ vocal dynamics as you speak, you make your stories and ideas come vibrantly alive for listeners.

The potential of your voice. One effective way to realize your vocal potential is simply to keep in mind that the voice is produced physically. That may sound obvious, but it's easy to forget when you're preoccupied with the content of your presentation.

Your voice is intimately connected to breathing, energy, and relaxation. So it easily reflects tension and stress. That means that the pressures of a too-hectic lifestyle or professional schedule will emerge in one form or another in your vocal expression. Anything you can do to relieve those pressures—yoga, sports, or relaxation exercises—will pay off in a more fluid and powerful vocal instrument.

Getting to flow. To be convincing as a speaker, you must combine the use of your voice with what you are saying. Beautiful words that don't sound meaningful will not convince anyone; but neither will the passionate delivery of a package empty of ideas.

The ultimate power and effectiveness of your content hinges not only on its relevance but also on your ability to sound committed to your ideas. When you fully commit to your message through a passionate delivery, your vocal presentation will achieve a natural flow that aids persuasion.

Delivering honesty. Once you're aware of your potential for vocal power, you can learn how to more subtly influence your audience. The suppleness of the vocal instrument is a factor presenters too often ignore.

The voice is the perfect tool to build trust; to instill confidence in a product, service, or idea; to create excitement among auditors; and to achieve many other positive outcomes. But for this level of change to occur in audience members, they must trust and respect you as a speaker. That means you must have an honest conversation with them, rather than "speechifying" or manipulating your message or listeners.

There are no tricks to influencing audiences. It all comes down—first, foremost, and finally—to honesty.

48: Like, Eliminating "Uh," "Um," and Other Vocal Fillers

Do you think you use the non-words "uh" and "um" too much in your speech?

Chances are, you don't.

These two non-fluencies—along with "like," "okay," "right," "you know," and even "so"—are examples of what communication experts term vocal fillers or vocalized pauses. Whatever you call them, they can be as annoying for speakers as for listeners.

But vocal fillers are hardly the biggest problem you'll face as a presenter. And anyway, the perception of the problem is usually worse than the reality. We tend to focus on these minor verbal tics the way we worry about the size of our ears or our nose. In other words, we give them greater importance than they usually deserve.

The other danger regarding vocalized pauses is that, somewhere along the line, someone mentioned that you say "uh" too much. From then on, every time you give a speech, all you hear is yourself saying "Uh" for what seems like a thousand times, and the rest of the speech disappears from your mind.

Believe me, this is not what your audience is focusing on! They are there to hear you say something of interest and importance to them, and getting that message across is what you should be alert to.

But if you insist on ridding your speech of vocal fillers, here are three ways you can do it:

1. **Discover the beauty of the pause.** Pauses in public speaking are lovely things. Used sparingly and wisely, pauses are powerful vocal tools that allow listeners to reflect on the important point just made. They also aid your speeches by helping to vary your pacing. A presentation without pauses is like a 100-car freight train going by at a railroad crossing: endless and boring. Listeners need a mental rest now and then. Pauses accomplish that.

    Speakers who pause also sound confident, since they're obviously not rushing to get the whole painful ordeal over with. Even better, pauses in a lengthy presentation are as refreshing as a sip of cool water on a sweltering day.

2. **Work with a tape recorder or video camera.** With any unproductive habit, first becoming aware of the problem is the critical step. So you may want to find out whether your vocal filler issue is as pronounced as you think it is.

    If you find that is the case, practice speaking into a tape recorder and then listening to yourself. At this stage, you'll hear practically nothing but your vocalized pauses. But give it time, and remember that it's not as bad as it sounds—you're only super-focused on the issue at the moment. Gradually, you'll improve. It's not a quick fix, but there really is no fast solution to this ingrained vocal practice.

3. **Enlist the help of a friend.** Have a friendly practice session in which a friend or colleague helps you with the problem. The person should listen to you speak while giving a cue each time you use your favorite vocal filler. The response can be visual,

such as raising the hand, or auditory—tapping on the table, ringing a small bell, that sort of thing.

Each time you hear the cue you must stop and start that sentence over. Personally, I would try the first two options before undertaking this one, because you might find it too frustrating. And for goodness sake, don't choose a member of your family to do this with!

49: Is Your Voice Helping or Hurting Your Career?

It's pretty obvious that what you say in a presentation matters more than the way you say it.

Right?

If you believe that, try reading the following short passages aloud. Speak them first in a flat monotone then with expression, as if this is the most important thing you'll say all year:

- "You may have heard that this company is washed up... finished. But I'm here to tell you: Acme Industries is not only going to win back our share of this sector—we're going to be the leader in this industry. And you're the people who can make that happen!"

- "The United States is absolutely committed to preventing further genocide, in this region or anywhere in the world."

- "I love you."

Did you find any differences in underlying meaning as you spoke neutrally or with emotion? Just as important: did *you* feel different the second time you spoke each passage?

Now read the short sentence below out loud. Actually, I want you to read the sentence six times, emphasizing one word in each instance. Start with the first word; then in your second reading, punch only the second word, and so on:

"I didn't give them those documents."

So what you just said was: "*I* didn't give them those documents"; "I DIDN'T give them those documents"; I didn't GIVE them those documents"; "I didn't give THEM those documents"; and "I didn't give them THOSE documents"; and "I didn't give them those DOCUMENTS."

You've just conveyed six different messages, haven't you?

The first exercise above (the three passages you read in a monotone and then with expression) makes use of emotional coloration in speech. The second exercise focuses on using emphasis to convey meaning. Together, they demonstrate a critically important point in public speaking:

Nothing gives you more opportunities to persuade listeners than the way you use your voice.

No other presentation technique is capable of such infinite variety. And nothing else you say or do can achieve such subtle shades of meaning and intention. Think about that: how often have you experienced the strength of what was said mostly from the way the speaker spoke the words?

In terms of your own career, invest some time to discover how effectively you use your voice. Come to terms with your abilities or shortcomings. Record yourself and listen to the sounds and intentions embodied in your voice. Try to grasp how others hear you, and then make decisions about you based on your voice. For they certainly do! Then start working on improving your problem areas.

When you give a presentation, include questions in your evaluation form that deal specifically with speech and voice issues. And try to locate a first-class speech coach, preferably someone with a background in acting.

Discover what your listeners already know about how your voice is helping or hurting your effectiveness as a communicator. Your professional success depends upon it.

50: The Two-Minute Speech Warm-Up

The Quick Tips in this chapter have been concerned with developing a flexible vocal instrument—a key skill for presenters. The voice, far more than any presentation asset you possess, is a *responsive* tool, one that only awaits your skill in using it.

Once you understand the profound ways in which your voice can affect listeners, you can use your instrument to elicit a wide range of colorations and effects. You can sound somber or lighthearted; cajoling or compelling; skeptical or inspirational. Having grasped the concept of vocal intentions, you can employ your vocal range and virtuosity to bring your important messages to life.

But as I've said earlier in this book, your voice is a physical mechanism. And like any other muscle group, it needs to be warmed up to function at peak efficiency.

Given today's hectic work and travel schedules (not to mention unrealistic speaking deadlines), getting a good workout can be a challenge. So here is a vocal warm-up that takes just two minutes. It covers three essential areas:

1. Breathing and resonance.

2. Supporting the sound.

3. Warming up the articulators.

Breathing and Resonance

- Close your eyes while standing. Take 3 slow deep breaths. Imagine your breath as both nourishment and relaxing energy.

- Focus on your abdominal area. Feel your abdomen come outward when you breathe in, and go in when you breathe out. This is healthy controlled breathing. It is diaphragmatic or natural breathing.

Supporting and Sustaining the Sound

- Now, breathing through the mouth, inhale slowly to a silent count of five. Pause your breath for a silent count of five; then exhale to a silent count of five. Do this three times.

- Choosing a comfortable pitch, produce the sustained sound "ahh" quietly and gently, without attacking the initial vowel.

Warming Up the Articulators

- Next, using your fingers, manipulate your facial muscles as if they were made of rubber. Practice chewing a huge imaginary wad of bubble gum, with your lips closed but your teeth apart. (Blowing imaginary bubbles is optional.)

- Stick your tongue out and rotate it in as wide a circle as possible (you might want to wait until your boss has left the area). Blow your lips outward in a floppy "horsey" sound.

- Now speak with exaggerated articulation any thoughts you like. Really allow your lips and jaw to move as much as possible. Repeat your vocalization(s) two more times with this exaggerated diction.

You're all set! You're now a) breathing diaphragmatically, b) controlling and sustaining the sound, and c) speaking crisply and with good articulation.

Knock 'em dead!

The Visual You: Body Language

"Your body [isn't] a way to get your head to meetings."

—SIR KEN ROBINSON

51: Body Language Secrets: What Self-Image Are You Broadcasting?

Visit a bookstore or search online for books on body language and you'll find a good selection on deciphering others' nonverbal cues. But why isn't there more on discovering what your own body language is broadcasting?

Certainly, the way you gesture, move, make eye contact, display facial expressions, and use proximity to those you interact with shapes their opinions of you. And nowhere is this truer than in the world of public speaking.

Let's look at how this interaction between you and those you want to influence plays out when you speak in public. For the inescapable truth is, your body language broadcasts to others who you are.

You may have heard the saying, for instance, "People are not persuaded by what we say, but by what they understand."

Talk about the importance of nonverbal communication! How you as a speaker use body language is a key skill in terms of the impact you have on stakeholders. These elements of your public speaking include your perceived level of confidence, leadership, and rapport with audiences.

Let's look at three specific ways audiences perceive you through your body language:

An Open (Confident) vs. Closed (Defensive) Personality: You alert audiences immediately as to whether you're a "closed" or "open" speaker. Clasped or locked hands create a barrier between you and the audience—a "safe" structure that you can hide behind. Similarly, hand gestures made with palms outward seem to be pushing the audience away. Relaxed and fluid gestures, on the other hand, tell listeners that you're confident. Equally important, they help create an impression of openness. That makes audiences more open to you in turn and more willing to be positively influenced by what you say.

Focused vs. Unfocused: When you present to any audience, you need to be 100% focused on your message and its reception. Everything you say or do needs to contribute to that end. When you're fully invested in what you're communicating, you'll naturally use your body unselfconsciously to amplify that message. Any absent-minded gesture you're in the *habit* of making can be a clear tip-off that you're unfocused and not really present for your listeners. Videotape yourself and you may be surprised by some physical habits you should leave behind!

Strong vs. Weak Self-Image: To be a confident and dynamic speaker who displays a strong self-image, you need to *command your performance space*. That's true whether that space is a conference stage, a pulpit, or anything in between. You need to maximize your physical presence, not minimize it. Give yourself this straightforward task: decide whether you shrink your physical presence when speaking or command your space. Again, practice in front of a mirror or a video camera. If you "apologize" for your physical presence through a too timid use of space, your influence will be correspondingly diminished.

52: The 6 Worst Body Language Mistakes of Public Speaking

One of my mantras that all of my clients hear is, "You have to get out of your head and into your body!"

That's because if there's a fundamental error that prevails in public speaking, it's the Talking Head Syndrome. Watch an exciting speaker who knows how to use physical expression, on the other hand, and you'll grasp how important a dynamic physical presence can be.

Below are six classic body language mistakes of public speaking. These errors are easy to commit and will significantly weaken your leadership and influence. I call them "the 6 worst" body language mistakes because of that level of importance and impact.

1. **Neglecting to Use Body Language in Public Speaking.** If you don't already incorporate physical expression in your talks, here's what I suggest: make some of your practice sessions specifically about movement. Walk around, swing your arms, and do anything you can to free yourself to use your body. Then rehearse realistically, noting the new freedom you've gained.

2. **Planning Movements Ahead of Time.** True physical expression in a speech or talk arises spontaneously. So you should never plan your movements. There's one exception: you can and should vary the spot where you deliver each important point you're making. But never script your speech in terms of body language, because it certainly will look that way in delivery.

3. **Moving Without Purpose.** "Suit the action to the word, the word to the action," Hamlet told the traveling players. In other words, make your actions appropriate to what you're saying. Do that, and there will be a *purpose* for the action. Don't take the motivational speaker approach and prowl the stage in an attempt to create excitement that doesn't otherwise exist.

4. **Failing to Command the Stage.** Looking and moving

confidently in public speaking is a clear mandate of leadership. Whatever the content of your message, your physical presence—your *stage presence*—needs to match your material in terms of impact. Make your movement, gestures, and overall level of energy *exactly large enough to reach the person farthest from you.* You'll create just the right "size" for your speech in terms of the audience and the venue.

5. **Not Amplifying Important Points with Gestures.** Do you think your words alone can convey meaning? Your gestures (along with your voice) exist to *amplify* and strengthen what you're saying. Try this simple experiment: Express out loud an opinion you hold strongly, but with your arms motionless by your side. Now say the same thing again, punching it with an appropriate gesture. You'll easily understand that creating the condition for the gesture, and allowing it to emerge naturally, will give your talks added vitality.

6. **Staying Tight.** Whenever you speak in public, you *show* your audiences how you feel about yourself and how you want them to think of you. So an audience is never to blame concerning the impressions they have of you. It's a mistake to stand like a statue or to make tight or overly timid gestures. Remember, just as emotions elicit physical responses (when you feel sad you cry), the opposite is true. When you *free* yourself through gestures, you'll actually feel comfortable and confident instead of nervous and tentative. You'll look to the audience like you're enjoying yourself—and they'll respond in kind.

53: Body Language and Leadership: 3 Ways to Command a Stage

Leaders speak, and speakers lead.

Whether you're contributing at a team meeting, presenting in a boardroom, or delivering the keynote at a national conference, if you're the one speaking, you're leading.

Or you should be.

Among the traits you need to speak for leadership are the physical aspects of your presentation. In other words, your performance skills are as important as anything you say.

And that means looking the part.

Audiences pay close attention and make important decisions based on what they see and hear. So here are three leadership skills of spoken performance that will strengthen your ability to captivate audiences. These approaches are all based in the techniques of the theater. They are *actor-based methods* that are the world's best tools for moving audiences. For that reason, they're custom-made for any leader's toolbox. After all, leadership is a performance skill, and adopting these practices will prime you for your own standing ovation when the curtain comes down.

1. **Move Fluidly and with Purpose:** Learn this essential lesson if you don't already know it: what an audience sees where you're concerned is how they'll judge you. Be the picture of self-assurance. Avoid awkward jerky movements, weak or repetitive gestures, or a deer-in-the-headlights quality on stage. All of those habits advertise self-doubt. Use gestures with intention, making each one clean and powerful. That is, when you use a gesture, make it count.

2. **Take Charge of Your Performance Space:** Your performance space is yours to command—however large or small that space is. You're a body moving in space; and your use of a stage is just as important as gestures where body language is concerned. Don't wander the stage or pace back and forth like a tiger in a cage. Instead, make your movement purposeful. And that lectern? Leave it behind and stand center-stage if you can. *That looks like leadership!*

3. **Create a Physical Expression of Your Message:** Think of this as your culminating skill, the capstone to your speech or

presentation. Ask yourself if you've *embodied* your speech, i.e., given it bodily expression rather than just delivering data. Every time you speak as a leader, it's your persona customers are buying more than anything else. When you think about it, physical expression is what public speaking performance is all about. Sending an email or a report is one thing. But a speech or presentation?… Ah, now you're talking!

54: Are You Exhibiting Nervous Body Language? — The Top 10 Signs

Have you noticed how many speakers seem to be on edge these days?

Actually, it's often just *nervous body language*. Whatever the reason, it can make an audience wonder why the speaker is adopting such odd behaviors. And they'll likely pay more attention to the sideshow than that speaker's message.

Here are some of the body language culprits that I (and perhaps you too) have been seeing recently. Be on the lookout for them if you want your own speeches to give the impression of a sleek sports car instead of a nervous wreck.

1. **Pacing.** This is the speaking style that more than any other gives audiences that I-feel-like-I've-just-run-a-marathon sensation. Speakers who are inexperienced and who long to make a splash love this technique. Remember, though, it's your ideas that should be exciting. Adopt a solid stance and let go: *stand and deliver,* and we'll get it.

2. **Wandering.** For audiences to retain your key messages, your movement has to be purposeful. Map out where you want to stand for each main point. This will help audiences retain your key items. For instance, three main points = three positions on stage. Easy!

3. **Fidgeting.** Here is nervousness literally personified. There are no specifically bad gestures to name here, and that's really the point. Random movements may keep listeners fascinated by your perpetual motion machine, but inattentive to what you're saying.

4. **Swaying.** Videotaping is a great way to have an out-of-body-experience and see yourself as audiences do. One habit you may notice is a tendency to sway. If you find yourself appearing to outlast a strong gale, you're a swayer. Tape, watch, and re-do to gradually gain control of your stance.

5. **Stepping Back-and-Forth.** This is purposeless movement in the opposite direction: backward and forward rather than side-to-side. It's another speaking habit you may be totally unaware of but that can drive audiences nuts! Again, a video camera or your smartphone will reveal the scene of the crime.

6. **Leaning to Port or Starboard.** This is yet another physical habit revealed by video that may amaze you. Leaning noticeably to the left or right will deprive audiences of a *visual representation* of your poise and steadfastness as a speaker.

7. **"Escaping" PowerPoint.** Have you seen this interesting body language tic? The speaker will glance back at the screen to be sure the right slide is displayed then flinch slightly when turning back to the audience. We all know that PowerPoint can be coma inducing; but can it actually attack the presenter?

8. **Retreating from Your Main Points.** In some talks, the speaker will step *backward* when bringing up each important point. It's a visible sign of nervousness in front of audiences. You should, of course, move *toward* listeners when you say something they need to know!

9. **Looking to Your Screen for Help.** Speakers who experience self-consciousness or anxiety often grasp at "life preservers." One of these can be their content, which seems familiar and safe. Why not retreat into familiar territory by looking at the screen to help

their explanations? But it's tough to convince people if you're not looking at them.

10. **Freezing.** Finally, body language nerves may manifest themselves not as extraneous movement, but no movement at all. Discomfort that freezes you in place is still a tip-off. A *disembodied* voice is great for horror movies, but it doesn't wear well on the public speaking stage. Again, get your body into the act.

55: Move! — How to Use Body Language to Tell Your Story

Recently, I coached a client who had a remarkable story to tell. It was a business team success story that had all the elements to gain an audience's interest. There was an urgent goal to be met and obstacles and challenges along the way. There were moments of uncertainty and despair. But finally, with the team working together tirelessly—and never doubting their purpose—there was triumph and joy at an extraordinary success.

So why wasn't this entrepreneur's success story as exciting as it could have been?

One reason was that I as the listener didn't *witness* the events unfold from his point of view. I don't mean in terms of visuals on a screen. I'm referring to his own involvement and emotional responses concerning the experience he was sharing with his audience. I'm speaking specifically here about the *physical expression* of his story.

And that, of course, means body language.

As speakers, we sometimes lose sight of an important fact: words and data may convey information, but nonverbal communication gives those facts greater meaning and significance. Our body language--including not only gestures but also facial expressions and our movement in the performance space—provides audiences with an observable physical dimension to what's happening in our story. It also gives them important emotional clues concerning that narrative.

Just like an actor, then, you must use your instrument—yourself—to get across what words, statistics, and other forms of evidence can't accomplish on their own.

Here are three ways you can make such an approach work for you.

First, use gestures that amplify or support your meaning. That's an easy-to-follow formula for dealing with the ever-present question, "What do I do with my hands?" Don't plan your gestures; instead, create the conditions in your own mind so that your gestures arise naturally. And make each gesture clean and definitive, without tentativeness or, if possible, too much repetition.

Second, use the *stage itself* as part of your story. Why simply stand there when the area surrounding you can help make your presentations more dramatic? If you think about the stage in a theater, you'll understand that "downstage" and "center," or "down-center" is the strongest position for you to deliver your introduction and conclusion, the most important parts of your talk.

Finally, plot your position on stage for each part of your speech. For instance, if you occupy a different place for each element of your story, your audience benefits from some visual variety. It's also easier for listeners to retain key points if you used a specific part of the stage to deliver each one.

What matters in the end is that you create a speech performance that's a physical as well as verbal expression of your message. Nothing is more compelling than a speaker who makes ideas come to life by physical means. It's called body *language*, after all.

56: Speaking with Power: Three Key Body Language Techniques

Want to speak with greater power while giving the appearance of complete confidence?

Here are three simple body language "tricks" for accomplishing those twin goals. Together, they'll give you more of the look of a leader while helping counter an excess of nerves or a too-low supply of public speaking boldness.

Trick #1: Ground Yourself in a Position of Power

First, learn how to ground yourself.

Grounding means to stand with both feet facing forward in a stable position. It's a strong, well-supported stance that lends you the look of a steady and steadfast speaker. Try it now: Stand with both feet touching; then with one leg crossed in front of the other; and finally in a "hip-shot" position with one hip thrust out. Now assume a *grounded stance*, with your feet parallel to each other at armpit width. Do you feel the difference in these stances in terms of your self-confidence and readiness to speak?

Trick #2: Open Your Upper Body So You Appear Confident

This body language trick comes straight from the world of acting. It involves opening your upper body to the audience.

When you speak in public, you have the same goal as an actor playing a major character: to demonstrate leadership in the context of your performance. A big part of that comes from your carriage, since that indicates how you feel about yourself. In other words, *how you stand affects your standing with an audience!*

Try standing two ways: first, allow yourself to get a little round-shouldered. Then consciously "open up" your chest area by straightening and ever so gently thrusting your chest forwards. Don't wrench your shoulders back though; just allow them to drop into place.

I bet you *feel* more self-confident! And there's no doubt whatever that you look more like a leader. Once you get the hang of it, you may decide never to go back to that slightly round-shouldered stance again!

Trick #3: Use Gestures to Add Strength to Your Messages

Finally, a word on using gestures to strengthen your messages. If you're wondering as many people do whether you use too many gestures, remember my simple rule: Any gesture that supports what you're saying is good, and any one that calls attention to itself or detracts from your message should be avoided.

But you should go further than that and use gestures to amplify the points you're making. To do so, start out in the "neutral position" with your hands at your sides. Start speaking from this position. (Yes, it may feel awkward at first, but it looks fine from the audience's point of view.)

Now bring your hands up and make a gesture only when you feel compelled to strengthen that point physically. Make the gesture clean, i.e., with some precision, and don't weaken it through repetition. Once you've used the gesture, let your hands return to your sides.

Two things happen when you do this: your gesture arises organically from the strength of what you're saying; and your hands are only noticeable *while you're making that point.* As you get closer to your actual speech, you can begin to loosen your control, adding more gestures so you're not too statue-like.

But if you start from the neutral position and use spare, clean gestures, you'll absolutely appear more in control. You'll seem comfortable speaking for leadership, and fully aware of how to make your points hit home.

Acting and Public Speaking

"All the world's a stage,

And all the men and women merely players;

They have their exits and their entrances,

And one man in his time plays many parts."

—WILLIAM SHAKESPEARE

57: The Actor's Art: What Can It Teach You About Public Speaking?

"A great actor can break your heart at fifty feet," said W.H. Auden. If there's a quote about acting worth knowing for public speaking, it's that one.

Every day, professionals in all sectors of our economy speak in meetings, presentations, pitches, lectures, keynotes, and interpersonal communication. And every one of these is a performance that's just as dependent on skillful speaking as a dramatic presentation.

Let's look at four major ways acting can help you create your own standing-room only performances when you take the stage.

#1 Actors Understand the Presentational Art

The reason live theater offers an immediacy that other

dramatic forms can't equal is that stage acting is a *presentational art.* Theatrical actors are carefully trained in the techniques of creating larger-than-life characters whose actions and personalities must fill an entire theater, in real time.

So too in public speaking: To communicate successfully with an audience, you must cultivate the ability to reach the person farthest from you—in this space, at this time. That means developing and projecting *physical expressiveness.* (See Chapter 9, "The Visual You: Body Language"). Whether it's gestures, facial expressions, eye contact, or your use of the stage, become comfortable in the art of presenting *yourself,* not just delivering information.

#2 Actors Know How to Move an Audience

Both common sense and neuroscience tell us that affecting audiences on an emotional level is a key to communicating successfully. And so you, like any actor, need the skills of reaching and moving listeners.

Emotions are more of the currency of public speaking than you might imagine. Even the most mundane decisions, science tells us, aren't possible without involvement of the emotional centers of our brains.

You may not be able to break the heart of audience members at fifty feet, but you must still touch listeners emotionally. Pour yourself into the things you believe most strongly, for passion compensates for many lapses in delivery skills. Business speakers in general keep themselves on too tight a leash. Allow your own passion to show, and you'll get an emotional response from listeners.

#3 Actors Can Externalize Thoughts and Feelings

You may have everything you need to be a great speaker in terms of deep expertise, commitment to your message, empathy, concern for listeners, and a fierce desire to deliver something of value. But it won't count for much if you can't get any of that across to an audience.

Like an actor, you need to be able to *externalize* what you're thinking and feeling. Audiences aren't mind readers. If you don't say, show, and demonstrate the importance and immediacy of what you're saying, how will they get it?

So the question becomes: Do you know how to use your instrument? Tape yourself on video to see how you externalize what you say in terms of body language, movement, facial expressions, and voice. Even better, work with a speech coach or take an acting class. Either approach will help you discover the connection between what you show and what your listeners receive and perceive.

#4 Actors Create the Illusion of the First Time

Do you speak frequently on the same topic? Make identical points in pitches? Use a stump speech with only minor variations?

However often you deliver key points or utter the same phrases, it can't sound that way to listeners.

Again, think of the theater. Stage actors lucky enough to be in a long run may be giving their 1,000th performance in a role—but they never lose sight of the fact that theatergoers may have paid $175 for their seat. And so they work hard every night at creating what's called "the illusion of the first time." The same dynamic applies to your presentations. However many times you've said the same thing, you must deliver it this time as though it's the first time.

Be like the actress playing a demanding three-hour role. She has a cold this evening and didn't sleep much last night. But as we all know, *the show must go on.*

Just like your presentation.

58: Stage Presence: Mastering the Art of Performance

What is stage presence, and is it required for public speaking? Google defines the term as "The ability to command the attention of a theater audience by the impressiveness of one's manner or appearance."

Do you need any of it as a speaker? Of course! Here are five elements of theatrical performance that apply directly to public speaking, with butterflies optional.

Element #1: Public speaking is a reflection of who you are. What often gets us into trouble in public speaking is the idea that it's something *special*—an out-of-the-ordinary event in which we need to perform spectacularly. But we're always performing, adjusting our demeanor based on the needs of the people and situation we're involved with at the moment. So make it your goal to connect with audiences, rather than trying to be excellent.

Element #2: Intentions and beats. When an actor plays a role, he or she is strongly focused on the *intentions* of the character. And when the character faces a changed condition that's a new beat. Theatrical beats equate with your main points as a speaker—for each new point you make should create a moment of renewed interest for your audience. You should therefore be aware of how your talk unfolds in these terms, and like an actor make each new main point look and sound different.

Element #3: Physical expressiveness. As speakers, we constantly run the risk of becoming talking heads. But our bodies are essential communication tools, from gestures to facial expressions to our proximity to the audience. To be the kind of speaker who commands attention, your speaking persona needs a physical dimension. Watch TED talks to get an idea of how some speakers enliven their speeches in this way while others remain static and uninteresting.

Element #4: Vocal dynamics for public speaking. Just as words have no physical dimension without your help, your beautiful language won't sing unless you give it voice. Keep this in mind: *Your voice is your most powerful instrument for creating in listeners the emotions you're feeling.* Remember, verbal is not vocal. Your words are one thing; the way you say them is something entirely different. Listen to Martin Luther King, Jr.'s "I Have a Dream" speech to get this.

Element #5: Using your performance space to command a stage. Do you think nonverbal communication means just posture, stance, and hand gestures? If you do, you're ignoring your need to use space productively and to command the stage. Just as the room itself plays a part in public speaking effectiveness, so too does the stage you're standing on. Use that space—the floor itself—as you move through your narrative and to bring you closer to the audience.

59: An Actor's Secrets: How to Improve Your Vocal Skills

When it comes to persuading, motivating, and activating audiences, you own one performance tool that's more important than all the others.

It's your voice.

Again and again in my work as a speech coach, I find myself explaining the vital role the voice plays in getting listeners to *feel* the power of what we say. Here are three ways you can use this unique tool of our species to humanize your own public speaking and make your presentations *sing*. Call this, three "e" tactics for improving your voice.

Encompass Your Listeners: Among its other attributes, the human voice depends upon physics to allow its message to be heard. That means making your voice audible, of course. But beyond this basic rule of being heard, you need to encompass listeners with your spoken sound. Think of it this way: audience members should feel as though you're standing next to them, with a friendly hand across their shoulder. It's intimate, you see. And the larger the space you're speaking in, the more important it is to try to achieve this effect.

How can you do that? Imagine an invisible bubble that encloses you, the person farthest from you, and everyone in between. Your job is to fill that bubble with your spoken voice. Everyone should not only hear you, but also have the impression that you're speaking to them individually. Don't try to achieve greater volume—instead, think of filling that shared space with a warm vocal presence.

Energize Your Audience: Let's stay with physics for a moment. Newton's Third Law says that "For every action, there is an equal and opposite reaction." An actively listening audience will be engaged by what you're saying, perhaps even excited by it. But for that to happen, you need to expend sufficient energy.

So if you want to energize your audience, start the process yourself with an upbeat vocal delivery. An under-energized voice dooms your message to an utter lack of distinction, power, and forward momentum. Your energetic voice, on the other hand, will achieve the opposite of all three of those outcomes.

Elicit Emotions: Now let's leave physics and enter the realm of human emotions. It's here, I believe, where the real power of our voices resides.

Your voice's true role is to *elicit in listeners the response to your ideas and emotions that you yourself experience.* The content of your presentation by itself can't accomplish that, by any stretch of the imagination. Your material may consist of data, argumentation, persuasion, supporting evidence, numbers, projections, and much else that's informative or fascinating. But you won't reach people on an emotional level unless they hear your total investment—your commitment—to what you're saying.

Encompassing listeners, energizing them, and eliciting the

emotions you want them to feel. Your voice—just like an actor's—will help make it all happen. So spend the time you need to use this marvelous, subtle tool to greatest personal and professional advantage.

60: Great Speaking? — It's About Performance Over Content!

Do you think your job is to deliver information when you give a speech or presentation? Too many speakers make that classic mistake.

Rather than making content your speaking focus, your task consists of something else entirely: it's to *influence* your listeners.

That may mean informing them, persuading them, activating them, inspiring them, reassuring them, or any of dozens of other purposes. But it's always the human connection that matters. You should be asking yourself, then: what are you going to do in this speech that will affect people enough to help improve their lives?

That's the reason public speaking depends so heavily upon *performance*.

So here's a simple formula for becoming a more exciting speaker: Instead of spending 100 percent of your time gathering content and 0 percent of your time practicing (as many speakers do), make the ratio closer to this:

Spend 40 percent of your time creating content, and 60 percent practicing.

Does that sound radical to you? If it does, remember this: you're already strong on your content. Your knowledge and experience are the reasons why you were chosen to speak. So the chances are you already have content coming out of your ears!

What you're probably lacking if you're a typical business speaker is a maximum level of comfort and performance skills relating to an audience. In fact, to be a truly excellent speaker, you should display a knack for conversing with audiences as if that were the most natural thing in the world.

So strengthen the area where you're probably weakest, for your strengths won't disappear in the process. Spend quality preparation time—and a quantity of it as well—learning to relate to audiences.

Practice the art of standing and moving naturally on a stage or performance space. Try out gestures, getting a feel for the ones that feel right and unforced and remain close to your body (avoid flinging your hands and arms out too far to the sides). Improve your eye contact by genuinely establishing a connection when you look at someone, and be sure to include listeners at the sides of the audience.

Just as important: learn to tell stories that will lend your content a human dimension. Some of those stories may come to you on the spur of the moment as you're discussing a topic. Trust them, and use them! Finally, train your ear so the voice you employ in formal presentations is as casual and expressive as the one you use with friends.

The more comfortable you become talking to groups of people, the more you'll feel like yourself, and the more you'll enjoy the speaking situation. That's when you'll begin to love your audiences as much as the content of your talks.

Guess how these audiences will respond.

61: Why Acting Matters in Your Business Presentations

Acting matters to your business career—and not only in terms of stage presence. In fact, it matters more than you realize.

There's the obvious reason, of course, that when you give a presentation, you're *performing*. But it goes deeper than that. The persona you show an audience is the essence of everything you display that goes beyond content. And that's a huge determinant of your success. In the end, it's the equal to whatever else your audience experiences. It's also a more direct route to the influence you're trying to achieve.

Let's look at how you already use the adoption of a stage persona in the acting performances you think of as your business presentations.

David Thomson, a writer on theater and film, published a book in 2015 titled *Why Acting Matters*. Actor and director Simon Callow discussed the book in a review in the *Wall Street Journal* titled "The Art of Persuasion." [1]

Thomson's book discusses acting and actors in terms of the public's ongoing fascination with the topic. But the book, and Callow's review, got me thinking along a slightly different line: why "acting matters" in business.

As an actor and speech coach, I'm interested professionally in the meeting place of public speaking and performance. Actors and business speakers, in fact, so often take part in the same activities—engaging, influencing, and moving audiences—that sometimes it's difficult to see daylight between the two.

There are differences, of course, including the most important one that actors play other people while business speakers play themselves. But the primacy of the performance itself in both cases can't be denied.

You, of course, play yourself when you speak professionally. But you work within the same paradox that actors do, in that you "wear" a speaking persona in your presentations that must still be rooted in your real personality. *That's* what makes you trustworthy and worth believing in the audience's mind. So that being true to whom you are when you give a speech provides both you and the audience with a beacon concerning the truth of that performance. Achieve that level of genuineness, and you won't have to worry about being "excellent."

To go for the glory, simply be you. After all, it's the performance of a lifetime.

---

[1] Simon Callow, "The Art of Persuasion," *The Wall Street Journal*, March 6, 2015

Engaging and Persuading Audiences

"I don't care how much a man talks, if he only says it in a few words."

—JOSH BILLINGS

62: Persuasion in Public Speaking Means Shaping Your Message

Achieving persuasion in public speaking is, as Hamlet said, "a consummation devoutly to be wished." Millions of speakers every day around the globe hope to accomplish that goal.

Persuasiveness isn't only the domain of a persuasive speech, however. In many instances, informative speeches—as well as inspirational talks, sales pitches, comments at meetings, and other speaking situations—include efforts to convince and achieve agreement.

Advice for being persuasive in public speaking isn't hard to find, either. But here I'd like to discuss an element of persuasiveness that often doesn't show up in tenets of persuasive speaking: the need to use effective transitions.

A simple realization should bring home why transitions are vital to clear and persuasive speaking: your audience doesn't know your talking points beforehand as you do. To convey your message so that listeners can follow where you're going, you need to make obvious connections between the points you're making.

Logic is the tool to bring to bear here. Since you conceived your presentation and know where your argument is going, you understand how the parts of your story fit together. But how will your audience see the connections unless you make them clear?

Intuitive leaps and self-evident links have no place here. You need to carefully lead your audience through what might otherwise be a thicket of information and causal relationships. Reminding them from time to time of the topic at hand, and referring back to a point you made previously are tactics that will aid your audience's comprehension. So will specifically mentioning how your previous point is related to the point you're about to make, through the use of internal summaries and previews.

Here's more on those two rhetorical devices: Let's say you're discussing a plan for increasing your company's profitability through a top-to-bottom makeover. You've laid out three main points in your opening concerning the actions that need to be taken: (1) better quality control, (2) improved distribution, and (3) more responsive customer service. You've just been talking about that first main point, greater focus on quality control. Now you're ready to discuss main point #2, distribution. Clearly, this is the first major transition of your talk.

Rather than saying (as some speakers do), "Now I'd like to talk about distribution," or pointing out (as even more speakers do), "Okay, the next slide is about distribution"—*you can use an internal summary combined with an internal preview,* like this:

"So I think you'll agree that better quality control will go a long way toward creating more satisfied customers." (Summarizing your previous point.) "But of course, great quality means little if you don't have a distribution system that quickly and reliably gets those products to market. That's the second element I'd like to talk about." (Giving listeners a "preview" of what you're about to discuss and relating it to your first main point.)

Solid transitions allow audiences to follow each point as it is logically and convincingly developed. Be strong in your transitions, and you'll be a leg up on speakers who have great content but don't give listeners a well laid out map to get to the destination.

63: Zombie Presentations: How Not to Speak like The Living Dead

Zombies. You gotta love 'em.

Like me, you may be a huge fan of *The Walking Dead.* Or perhaps you laughed and screamed your way through *Shaun of the Dead,* or thrilled to the amusement park scene in *Zombieland.* From *Abraham Lincoln vs. The Zombies,* to *Zombies! Zombies! Zombies!* we can all appreciate good zombie fare (though probably not at dinnertime). And boy, are these lovable stiff-walkers popular: Wikipedia lists 660 zombie films!

Zombie business presentations, however, are another matter. If you find yourself thinking that one of the undead is delivering the speech or presentation you're listening to, it's because a few basic rules are being ignored. To keep from finding yourself in such a horror-inducing situation when you're the one behind the lectern, follow the 5 tips below.

1. **Speak to other living things.** Let's face it: zombies don't relate well to the still living. And they'll do anything to avoid talking to them. In a zombie's universe, inanimate objects are much safer sources of their attention while they're speaking (unless they haven't chewed on an arm or a leg for four hours or more). Manuscripts, note cards, PowerPoint screens, their shoes, the ceiling, and even the back wall are popular destinations for a zombie's gaze. So avoid the Undead Stare and look at your listeners, making a connection as you discuss the things you share an interest in. Your talk will come to life! (If it wasn't there already.)

2. **Reanimate your voice.** If your voice sounds like it barely made it back from the grave, it's time to consider some speech improvement. A lively and engaging voice depends upon five key tools: 1) energy and emphasis, 2) pitch inflection, 3) varied pace or rate, 4) pauses and silence, and 5) vocal quality. Dynamic speakers use all five of these tools; zombies, vampires, and other varieties of the-no-longer-living simply don't. Try engaging a werewolf in lively Q & A following his or her presentation and you'll immediately see what I mean.

3. **Shock your heart back to life.** You may not realize this during a heart-stopping scene of zombies chasing your movie hero, but your heart doesn't actually stop. A zombie's heart, however, has. Which means they are absolutely lousy at using emotion to move an audience. That's because not only persuasive speaking, but also informative speaking and every other type of presentation has an emotional component. You have to reach your audience's hearts and minds. So it's helpful to ask yourself if there's an emotional element to the speaking situation you're a part of. And consciously use emotional language to engender the response you're looking for. Believe me, if your audience doesn't see something beating in your chest, they may start chasing you through the streets.

4. **Don't move like a corpse.** Did you know that the theory of embodied cognition states that movement itself helps you think? No wonder zombies stink at conveying their messages— they move like blocks of wood with legs! Added to this is the fact that an audience needs visual variety during a speech. Body language (and here I mean movement from live bodies, not dead ones) can also help audiences engage with you and retain your key points if you move to different parts of the stage. Using appropriate movement and gestures is an exciting area of public speaking effectiveness. Learn to do so now, while you're still breathing.

5. **Talk—don't grunt!** You know what this sounds like: the speaker peppers his or her speech with "uh," "um," "like," "you know," and "UUUUUUH... NEED BLOOD!" These examples of non-fluent speech are called vocalized pauses or vocal fillers. Zombies make these sounds because their mouths are filled with dirt, worms, and sometimes, chipped teeth if they've chewed their way through a tombstone. But you're probably not in that situation when you speak, right? If you find yourself using vocal fillers too frequently, practice with a tape recorder or smartphone. Don't videotape yourself because you'll be seduced by the visual. If all you have to pay attention to is your voice, you'll gradually improve in eliminating these utterances that are nothing but well, dead air.

64: How to Read an Audience and Think on Your Feet

One of the skills of a consummate presenter is the ability to think on one's feet. After all, anyone can give a competent presentation provided they know their material and have practiced enough. But what happens when challenging questions and objections raise their heads? Or suppose you're asked to reason your way through a thorny hypothetical situation when you thought you had all the bases covered?

Rather than fear such situations, you should welcome them. For the fact is, these are precisely the occasions that prove your worth as a speaker. If you can grapple with tough questions while retaining a mastery of your subject, your persuasiveness, credibility, and influence with audiences will soar.

It's no wonder then that one of the principal tasks of a speech coach is to help presenters think on their feet.

So how is it accomplished? It's done by bringing not only a fierce level of concentration to your task but also a high level of awareness of what's happening around you. Don't be like the oblivious speaker who buries his nose in his manuscript, or the pompous attorney who reads her entire opening statement from a yellow legal pad.

Instead, be completely present and paying attention. A powerful presenter is exactly like the major league baseball player who finds himself up against the league's best pitcher. Both must bear down with 100% attention to what's coming their way. Here are two ways you can achieve that level of focus on task:

1. **Listen with your whole being.** Open yourself up completely to the nonverbal communication your audience is sending your way. That means using all of your senses. For some of us, this involves getting over ourselves so that we can be fully present for listeners.

    Watch how people are reacting to what you're giving them. Pay attention not only to what they say, but how they sound when they say it. Mark their physical response. Especially make sure your antennae are out to receive their emotional reaction. By responding in these ways, you'll be fully present to a degree you may not have imagined possible. Listeners will not only be impressed; they'll be amazed because few public speakers are this attentive to the audience.

2. **Expect a reaction.** Most of the time, audience members won't react to what you're saying. Audiences are preconditioned to be passive and unresponsive. Even people who are intensely interested in your topic won't show it outwardly. But you should speak as if you could get a reaction from anyone in the audience any moment now.

    Being that focused and ready will keep you fresh and looking responsive in real time. When you do get an externalized reaction, you'll be able to respond to it instantly. Just as important, you'll be demonstrating an honest presentation style that shows you're right there with your listeners every step of the way.

65: More Thinking on Your Feet: One-Minute Impromptus

Ready to really challenge yourself in terms of thinking fast and speaking eloquently? Use an exercise I created for my coaching clients I call "One-Minute Impromptus."

The task is simple but devilishly challenging. I tell the client he or she will have one minute to take notes on a topic I'll give them, before speaking for one minute. A stopwatch or timer on my smartphone keeps both of us honest.

Of course, I choose a topic related to their work or the type of speaking they do so the exercise is helpful for their upcoming talks. For people who pitch business or routinely face tough audiences, One-Minute Impromptus is a natural skills- and confidence builder.

It doesn't always seem that way at first. It's interesting, for instance, how often a client will say when the one-minute beep sounds: "But I didn't get to my topic yet!"

In Round 2, they'll generally do better. We'll go through the exercise three, four, even five or six times in a row, videotaping and debriefing each time. And it's always amazing how quickly the person learns to achieve greater clarity and conciseness in a brutally short period of time.

You can play the game yourself by writing out your topics beforehand and placing them in an envelope. If you've let a sufficient amount of time go by before you go back to those topics, you'll have forgotten the challenging queries or thorny scenarios you wrote down.

In other words, you'll have a nice supply of topics as you wrestle with this tough but eye-opening exercise in becoming a speaker who can think on your feet!

66: Ask Many Small Questions... Okay?

Have you heard that a rhetorical question is a great way to get an audience's attention? Well it is. The reason is simple: listeners respond mentally to questions, whether or not they think a vocalized answer is expected.

Don't you agree?

Questions are custom-made speech tools for bridging the gap between audience passivity and a speaker's need to actively engage and persuade listeners. The problem is that audiences are conditioned to be passive recipients of information: to sit quietly while information washes over them. As the Eagles song "Hotel California" says: they are programmed to receive.

But human beings learn poorly in the passive mode. They retain much more information when they are active participants in the learning process. An endless procession of PowerPoint slides, for instance, can be more coma inducing than enlightening.

Questions bring listeners back from this netherworld. Remember the times when you were daydreaming in class and you suddenly heard your name called? That focused your mind pretty quickly didn't it?

Rhetorical or not, questions invite your audience to reacquaint themselves with you and what you're saying. But there's no need to wait for make-or-break responses to your major points. Even in a 30-minute presentation, there will be dozens of times when you can "ask small questions" to re-engage your audience. Here are some common examples:

"Isn't that so?"

"Haven't you found that to be the case?"

"You know what I'm talking about don't you?"

"Yes?"

"Yes or no?"

"We've all experienced that haven't we?"

"Right?"

"Everybody with me so far?"

Any questions?

67: Why Audiences Want to See You Naked (and Why You Should Be Glad)

Are you an acknowledged authority or expert in your field?

If you are, that's nice. But it's not enough to be fully persuasive in public speaking.

Many are the movers and shakers, experts all, who fail to connect emotionally with listeners and convince them of the real message they are there to convey.

Knowledgeable people don't usually lose their jobs because of a bad speech. But they often fail to reach their full potential as influencers. Especially for super-achievers in this group, realizing that they lack the ability to come across as vibrant and entertaining can be a disagreeable proposition.

Why does this happen? I think it's a left-brain/right-brain problem.

Left-brain analysis and logic can take you far, especially in highly empirical fields like finance, engineering, medicine, or the sciences. But when it comes to being influenced by speech, it's the right brain that's working overtime in listeners' minds.

Successful talks not only persuade people, but also change the minds of listeners in some fashion. And that's a process that's strongly driven by right brain emotional responses. You can't be a dynamic communicator, in other words, unless you know how to touch people emotionally.

But there's no need to run out for a quick Ph.D. in psychology. Simply remember that the ability to move audiences begins with honesty, and that everything flows from this starting point. That means being fully present in speaking situations. It also requires dealing with listeners on a human-to-human basis, rather than speaking from on high or being more concerned with data than people.

Of course, you must pay attention to how listeners are receiving information so you can switch gears if necessary. But you must also take chances, staying open and vulnerable rather than going for cheap effects. As a starting point, listen to your voice (record yourself if necessary) responding to tough questions or criticisms from audience members.

You may find that your nakedness in a public speaking situation is a frightening scenario. But it's always more interesting for an audience than a cover-up.

68: How to Move an Audience to *Action*

Getting your audience to actually do something after you persuade them—or to change their thinking, which is just as challenging a proposition—is a key ingredient to successful public speaking. Yet it is all too easy for us to become overly focused on the content of our presentations and to miss the actionable part completely. That's because we're usually doing our best to keep people interested, instead of asking ourselves: "How can I activate them?"

And anyway, "interested" is a state of mind and nothing more. We must ask ourselves instead how we want to affect listeners, to leave them better off than they were before. Such thinking requires a different type of planning on our part.

We take a huge step up by thinking along these lines—from merely delivering information to getting our audiences to behave differently as a result of our having spoken. The mechanism for accomplishing this isn't complicated: You simply need to ask yourself what you want listeners to think, feel, or do as a result of your speech. With that change in your own thinking, you'll begin walking a path that should yield much more tangible results.

Here's an example of how this works:

Let's say you're scheduled to give a speech on the need for co-ordinated global action to reduce climate change. Interesting? Yes. Important topic? Sure. But your speech can engage and motivate listeners in many different ways depending on the action you're seeking from the audience. For instance:

- Do you want them to analyze a specific aspect of the problem?
- Write a letter to the editor of their local paper?
- Sign a petition to the state legislature?
- Buy a more fuel-efficient car?
- Begin recycling?
- Start an Earth Day awareness campaign in their town?
- Ride public transportation one day a week?
- Make a financial contribution to your organization?
- Buy a hybrid vehicle?
- Start a legal advocacy group?
- Stop using spray deodorant?

The degree of action you want from listeners will depend in part on a shift in your own thinking and planning for your speech. That is, the level of action you require of listeners will dictate your approach, tone, organization, forms of evidence, degree of fervor, and numerous other factors concerning how you structure and deliver your presentation.

Once you understand exactly how you want the audience to react, you'll begin to think in terms of the tools and approach you can use to make that happen. Factors will include the stories you bring into your presentation, along with the emotional tone and sense of immediacy you establish. You'll be practicing two essential components of speeches that aim for action: thinking and speaking strategically.

69: Curtain Up! Add Drama to Your Speeches

When was the last time you sat through a truly memorable presentation? I'm talking about a speech with fresh ideas and true feelings, movingly delivered, with a clear and exciting sense that the topic really mattered.

Perhaps you've never experienced a presentation like that. If you have, the odds are excellent that you remember it. And one reason you do may be because the speaker had a sense of drama.

As you conceive your own presentations, ask yourself where the drama exists in your talks. Drama moves audiences like nothing else in the world. Speeches with drama deal with human beings facing challenges and conflicts—which are to say, the times when they're most interesting—and finding ways to overcome those limitations.

Look back on your own life and determine where the drama lies. For all of us, it's easier to understand the power that a dramatic story can pack through the events of our own life.

Now transfer that sense of highs and lows to your product, service, mission, or whatever else your topic may be about. Who was facing defeat but won? Who took the bravest chance and prevailed? Think power, conflict, heroes, quests, adventures, underdogs, dark deeds, white steeds, and against-all-odds triumphs. These are the ingredients of drama.

And don't imagine these things exist only in fairy tales and action films. The story you want to tell is filled with them. They're the stuff of struggles and successes on behalf of people in need, including customers, clients, and constituents. You know all about that, don't you?

So start digging for that gold.

70: Speaking Visually in the Age of Television

Do you know what the greatest persuader in the world is?

It isn't a person.

It's television.

Over the past half-century, television has fundamentally transformed public discourse and altered the way we respond to critical information. It has accomplished this by teaching us that important information always comes with some kind of visual reinforcement.

Think of the evening news. We see a few seconds of the news anchor telling us what today's top story is then we immediately go to a video showing us what's happening. If we were to watch a news-broadcast from, say, the early 1960s, we'd probably be shocked at how static it all seems, with too much talking by the anchor without anything visual to spice up our experience.

The implication of all of this for speeches is clear: Presentation excellence in the 21st century requires a strong visual component to accompany the words.

In fact, it isn't only television that's changing our perceptions. Video games, smartphones, Apple watches, and shape-shifting billboards are doing their part daily, even minute-by-minute.

Audience members, in other words, are already awash in a sea of visual information. And since they seem to be swimming along splendidly, we'd better learn how to put our speech-oars in the water.

Fortunately, as presenters we already have considerable visual resources at our disposal. Most important among these, perhaps, is ourselves. We truly are our most effective visual aid.

Another highly effective visual component to speeches and presentations is stories. For as we'll see below, stories offer rich possibilities to use the visual elements that today's audiences crave.

I mentioned in Quick Tip #15 that stories show us at our most personable and communicative. They also present the perfect opportunity to speak in visual terms, since they unfold as a series of pictures in listeners' minds. Novelists discovered in the last century how to mimic the cinematic-inspired visual unfolding of a story. We presenters need to learn how to do likewise.

Slide technologies and other visual presentation tools offer us one way to do so. But an equally effective tactic is to create "word-pictures" in the minds of audience members. For instance, note the difference in the following two openings of a speech on globalization:

Opening A: "Good morning. I'm delighted to be here with the representatives of the Pan-American Trade Council. This conference reinforces for me the rapid progress your country has made recently in its efforts at globalization. The statistics clearly show how many more of your indigenous goods are available in the global marketplace."

Opening B: "Good morning. What a delight to be here on behalf of the Pan-American Trade Council—and what a reminder of how much your beautiful country has to contribute to that relationship. On the drive in from the airport, we passed one of your farmers markets. And I must say, I was amazed at the variety of goods I saw for sale!

There was handmade clothing in vibrant local patterns, rows of brightly painted ceramics, and the luscious colors of the tropical fruits. For me it was a powerful reminder that your country truly has much to offer the global marketplace."

When we speak visually, we conjure up vivid representations in the minds of audience members. Not only that; but such imagery allows listeners to construct their own personal visuals out of the experiences of their lives—for no one can visualize what they haven't seen for themselves, at least in part, at some point. When

I ask you to visualize a tornado, what you see in your mind's eye is what you have seen at some point in the past.

Almost no other technique besides painting word pictures like this allows you to reach that level of personalization and emotional connection with listeners. And don't forget that decisions—including being persuaded—take place in the right brain, the hemisphere most concerned with spatial relationships.

Picture how important all of this is for you as a speaker.

Dealing with Skeptical Audiences and Resistance

"The secret of being a bore is to tell everything."

—VOLTAIRE

71: Know Your Listeners' Needs and Expectations

Understanding who your listeners are and what they expect from you is essential to persuading them. This knowledge is particularly useful for audiences who are skeptical or resistant to your message.

If that's the case, ask yourself the following four sets of questions beforehand. The answers will benefit you with any audience, but they will be especially helpful with skeptical or resistant groups of listeners:

1. **Who are you trying to influence in this presentation?**

   - Is it the people actually in the room or auditorium?

   - Is it instead bosses, board members, or other opinion leaders not present?

   - Are there other behind-the-scenes decision makers to be concerned about?

   - Should your primary influence be aimed at representatives of the media?

   - Is speaking to the community at large the smarter move at

this point?

- Are there political considerations that supersede your content?

The central question with the above considerations is this: Are the people present the ones you really need to convince, or is it someone else?

2. **What do these people know and expect in this speaking situation?**

- What is the audience's knowledge of your topic?
- How much essential information should you be trying to get across? (Avoid an information dump, especially if listeners are already familiar with aspects of your topic!)
- Do these listeners have clear expectations concerning your presentation?
- What are their preferences concerning presentation style, and their level of engagement and participation?

Here, you need discipline! You must speak at the appropriate level of knowledge providing only the amount of information needed. Do your homework. Can you obtain information about previous presentations to this group? What did those speakers do? Were their efforts successful? Why or why not?

3. **What is the emotional context of the occasion?**

- Is there any bias toward or against you, your topic, or your organization?
- Are the attendees here voluntarily or not?
- Is there an emotional climate prevalent that you should know about? (Examples include an industry crisis, a significant company milestone, a recent change in leadership, etc.)
- Do cultural issues apply?
- Are your *values* or those of your organization important to this audience?
- How easy or difficult is the action you're asking the audience

to take as a result of your presentation?

Emotions and values can be critical factors in your success as a speaker, and so you ignore them at your peril. Does this audience have a worldview that is central to their reception of your message? Has anything occurred in their world recently to positively or negatively impact their receptivity?

4. **How will your message benefit these listeners?**
    *   What is the relationship of your topic to their professional or personal lives?
    *   Will you include practical knowledge or skills they can use immediately?
    *   Will your talk foster group cohesion and motivation?
    *   Is your goodwill completely evident to them?

Your listeners must believe that you are speaking for their benefit not your own. Is that message getting through to the audience loud and clear?

72: Understand the Culture You're Dealing With

What associations does the word *culture* elicit in your mind in terms of an audience? For many of us, a culture refers to a clearly defined geographical, historical, or national grouping: the Bedouin, Tibetans, the cowboys of the American West, etc.

Ruth Fulton Benedict, a cultural anthropologist, had this to say about this interpretation of culture:

From the moment of his birth the customs into which [an individual] is born shape his experience and behavior. By the time he can talk, he is the little creature of his culture.

— *Patterns of Culture* (Boston: Mariner Books, reissue ed., 1989)

Whole libraries exist on communicating within this definition of culture—books concerning gestures and taboos, global business practices, and protocols required for social and professional interaction. If you conduct business internationally, or you're a diplomat, social services volunteer, or are called upon to give speeches abroad, this is an area in which you would do well to educate yourself.

But many *audience* cultures exist that have nothing to do with geography or political bonds. These are often sub-cultures within a larger population. The cultural categories can be large—religious, racial, occupational, gender—or more finely differentiated: a social network, a club or fraternal order, a collection of hobbyists, or simply a group of interested individuals.

Companies and organizations have their own sub-cultures as well. A speech to the sales department of a large corporation will probably require a different approach than one to compliance officers of the same company.

The expectations of well-defined groups can differ dramatically where a speaker is concerned. Sometimes that difference will impress itself upon you as merely an interesting homogeneity of thought and action. But at other times a palpable resistance may be evident.

When speaking to cultures that are different from your own, try to understand as accurately as possible the expectations of your audience. In broad cultural categories, this may mean simply respecting hierarchies and levels of authority. In more finely sliced cultural categories, however, succeeding often comes down to understanding the specific likes and dislikes of the group and the mechanics of the presentation itself.

Does this audience prefer a lecture or interactive exercises instead? Do they want down-in-the-weeds details, or should you fly at 30,000 feet, offering a more expansive view that reveals your overall vision? Does this group enjoy open-ended discussions, or does that prospect horrify them?

Ask yourself if this gathering is likely to be respectful to you and your approach, or more aggressive in responding to your message. Then consider how you will deal with either outcome.

Perhaps most important, make sure you strongly establish your own credibility. Mention your credentials, experience, or accomplishments as early as possible. And don't shy away from referring to departments within the organization you've had dealings with or influential individuals you've worked with whose names listeners may recognize.

Since you're not a member of this culture, your audience will need persuading concerning why they should listen to you. Give them solid reasons at the start, when they're making critical judgments about you.

73: Seven Tips for Overcoming Audience Resistance

Quick Tips #71 and #72 above discuss ways to understand your audience's knowledge, expectations, and cultural biases. They offer guidance for overcoming resistance by helping you strategize and prepare beforehand for the types of groups you may be facing. Now I'd like to discuss resistance that you can't anticipate: the kind that rears its head during your presentation.

The first thing worth understanding concerning challenges from an audience is that you shouldn't fear them. Salespeople understand that quibbles—and even clear disagreements—are often necessary steps toward a successful sale. It's the same with presentations and the audiences that hear them.

For one thing, questions and objections mean that listeners remain engaged with you and your topic. They haven't shut themselves off and stopped listening to your argument. That's a critical point in your favor.

Resistance is a natural element of thinking and attentive audiences. Therefore as speakers we mustn't run away from it. We lose a considerable part of our persuasiveness when we adopt a "siege mentality," believing that our job is to continually dodge flaming arrows that are hurtling our way over the battlements.

The instant we shift from reaching out toward listeners to defensiveness, we lose control of the situation, and it shows. From that point on, we've stopped advocating effectively on behalf of our message.

So stay positive and hopeful! Audiences generally respect a speaker who stands up for his or her beliefs in the face of determined resistance. Here are seven practical ways you can gain that respect and still deliver your message effectively.

1. **Understand the type of resistance you're facing.** Is it institutional or personal? Fact-driven or cultural? An ego trip for the questioner, or a flaw in your logic? *Be alert to what's coming your way, but respond honestly.* Your credibility with listeners will stay strong and perhaps even improve.

2. **Listen for emotions.** My emotional state as an audience member can be a major reason why I'm resisting your message. You represent a point of view, a company, the accepted way of doing something, etc. Therefore, you provide a convenient target for me to attempt to redress a recent problem or to vent after decades of resentment and anger. There may also be subtle connotations in what I say to you as speaker that you would do well to listen for, so that you can respond appropriately.

3. **Recast erroneous assumptions.** The more damaging an erroneous assumption expressed by an audience member, the sooner you must publicly correct the error. This may even mean interrupting the questioner. It can be done nicely ("Excuse me, but I can't agree…"). But it's vital that you set the record straight as soon as possible. Otherwise, the faulty argument sits in the minds of the audience, slowly setting like concrete.

4. **Welcome unclear or fuzzy arguments.** Yes! If the logic of your opponent is faulty, or her argument is simply so much

debris floating in the vastness of space… you win! Accept this gift, and use the objection to take your response in any direction you choose. You may, for instance, state the strongest argument in support of your case all over again.

5. **Go low-key and conversational.** The more an audience member attempts to provoke an emotional response from you, the quieter you should become. Take your time in answering his argument, be logical, patient and if possible, kind. Your soothing nature will compare favorably with your opponent's volcanic personality.

6. **Be aware of your tone.** As stated above, incorrect assumptions and damaging assertions must be countered immediately. But the best arguments in the world will fail if you sound defensive or angry. *Listeners will remember the tone of your response far more strongly than your facts and statistics.* Remember, a huge component of the message that's ultimately received by audiences resides in your tone alone!

7. **Disagree neutrally.** Many opportunities will arise with difficult audience members for you to demonstrate your rapier wit. Resist every one of them, for the reasons given above.

74: Be a S.A.N.E. Speaker

As speakers, we like to think we'll have a positive effect even when listeners are resistant. The sobering reality however is that very few presenters achieve such influence. Most talks and speeches are just like all the other talks on that issue. They show little creativity or boldness. And so they fail where the crucial requirement of influencing listeners is concerned.

So what can we do as speakers to establish rapport and reach listeners in some actionable way despite skepticism and resistance? We can remain S.A.N.E., by remembering to do the following:

Shape the issue: You give yourself a tremendous advantage as a speaker when you frame your message in ways that work to your advantage. In fact, it's difficult to overcome skepticism and resistance unless you do so.

Consider the example of a classic management-labor dispute. Union leaders invariably present the issue as either a) a "fair shake" for the workingman and -woman, or b) a case of Big Business vs. the little guy. (Often they use both arguments simultaneously.)

Company officials typically will raise the question of fairness as well, by asking a question such as: "Are the union's demands fair compared to what ordinary Americans are getting in terms of wages and benefits?" Or they will frame the situation in even starker terms, warning that the company won't survive if the union's demands are met. Both sides in a labor-management dispute thus consciously try to shape the issue to their own advantage.

Areas of agreement: Your influence with a resistant audience depends partly on whether you can establish common ground with them. And the earlier you do so, the better.

Once audiences understand that you and they are working toward a common goal, they'll be much more likely to view you as a person with integrity. This is important especially if your views differ significantly from theirs. You'll at least be a speaker who's worth listening to. Who can ask for more than that?

New approaches: People who resist your point of view will be convinced they've already heard all the arguments on your side. So surprise them. Give them something they haven't heard before.

It needn't be a radical departure from past presentations, though it might be. At any rate, focus on stories and metaphors as you make your case. Above all, use comparisons your audience can understand.

An audience of salespeople I once trained, for instance, was delighted to hear that *silence* was as important in persuading a prospect as anything they said. (They understood that customers often need a few seconds for a critical point to sink in.) I used the comparison of Zen masters who tell us to look at the space between objects instead of the objects themselves. From their point of view, it was an unexpected but apt comparison. Of course, this means that you need to do your homework to understand who your listeners are and how they think.

Emotions: We hold the beliefs we do because we think they are the right beliefs, the ones that correspond to our values. And that involves a strong emotional component. If you want to change people's convictions or behavior, you won't do it with statistics and pie charts. You have to speak about your issue in ways that touch people's lives.

Don't be afraid to reveal, for instance, how you have wrestled with this issue. You'll be giving them permission to do the same, and perhaps come out of the struggle on your side of the equation.

75: Defuse Your Opponents' Arguments

When we hear the word "argument," we often think of disagreement and contentiousness. Yet the first definition of argumentation in my office dictionary is "the process of arriving at reasons and conclusions."[1]

The process of arriving at reasons and conclusions. What a different meaning from the commonly understood one concerning "argument"! And what an opportunity to use the tools of logic and evidence discussed elsewhere in these pages.

For if influencing listeners depends upon making the better argument—as it does in everything from advertising to politics—then recognizing and countering your opponents' line of reasoning can be a critical factor in your success.

You might say it's a process of defusing your opponents' "bombs" before they can be thrown at you.

---

[1] David B. Guralnik, editor in chief, *Webster's New World Dictionary* (New York: Simon and Schuster, 1980), 74.

Lawyers certainly understand this. If there's a skeleton in their client's closet, and the opposing side knows about it, the attorney will often drag it into the open first in direct questioning rather than letting it emerge in hostile cross-examination. The theory is that a weakness you reveal yourself will do less damage than it will when trumpeted by your enemies.

Similarly, when an organization is in the midst of a crisis, the worst thing it can do is to withhold damaging information so that it leaks out, drip by corroding drip. Everyone knows that it wasn't the burglary itself but the cover-up that brought down the Nixon administration.

The same advice holds for you as a speaker. By raising your opponents' objections first, you can deflate them with the argument you've prepared beforehand. That's almost impossible to do with, say, a question from the audience that blindsides you.

You've often heard experienced speakers use this tactic. It may sound something like this: "The other side says we shouldn't take this course of action. But let's look at what would happen if we were to follow the risky plan they've put forward."

So think of the strongest or most likely objections to your position, including those from audience members you expect to be resistant. Then come up with *your most powerful case to prove those arguments wrong.* Employ the principles of evidence, reasoning, emotion, logic, storytelling, and lively delivery.

If you're successful, you may hear that most beautiful of sounds: minds changing.

Phone Conversations and Conference Calls

"The telephone ... has a romance of its own."

—VIRGINIA WOOLF

76: Why Your Voice Matters in Phone Conversations

How important is the sound of your voice on the phone? When you speak in person, your voice is a contributing factor to how people perceive you and your intentions, of course. But in the case of phone conversations, well, your voice *becomes* your speaking persona in the minds of listeners.

So you're taking a considerable risk by ignoring the qualities you project vocally over the phone. Let's look at some of the factors that are at play when you're in a call or phone conference, and how you can use them to improve your skills and impact.

First, understand that *your voice rules when visuals are absent.* In spite of our increasingly visual experiences—from television to movies to the Internet to texting to video games—a huge component of our world still depends upon what we hear.

Consider this fact as well: according to the experts, oral communication preceded writing by around 45,000 years! And sure as you can grunt in agreement, nonverbal communication arrived before anything verbal. That means your listeners are hard-wired to respond to the vocal cues you're giving them apart from the words you're using. I think of this purely vocal influence as a fast-flowing river of influence running underneath everything we're saying.

And in any conflict between nonverbal communication and verbal content, nonverbal communication wins. Think of the CEO asked by a financial reporter if the company's stock will rebound next year. "Absolutely!" he replies, *shaking* his head. Now consider the same conversation on the phone: though the CEO *says* he's confident, the lack of conviction in his voice may give exactly the opposite impression. Once again, nonverbal communication has overruled what was said.

The result in both cases is a listener unconvinced by the words being spoken because the nonverbal clues offered are saying something else.

Paul Ekman, the world's foremost researcher into facial expressions and emotions, has even educated us about "micro expressions"—fleeting arrangements of our facial muscles that last for only a fraction of a second but reveal the true feelings and intentions of the speaker. [1]

Now think about the phone conversations and conference calls that may be an everyday part of your professional life. Most of the time, visuals are missing in these encounters. And in the absence of any rich visual clues, listeners will focus strongly on your voice. So if you don't have control of your nonverbal expressiveness and know how to use your voice effectively, you'll be short-changing yourself in terms of accomplishing your goals.

Below are half a dozen strategies for proceeding in the opposite direction.

---

[1] Learn more about micro expressions in Ekman's book *Emotions Revealed.*

77: Six Strategies for Improving Your Vocal Presence on the Phone

1. **Vocal Quality:** Write out the characteristics you want your voice to embody. Absent an acting course, you've probably never had the opportunity to explore the flexibility of your voice. Go ahead and do so now. Record an ordinary sample of what you talk about on the phone, and check it against that list of favorable characteristics.

2. **Posture:** Sit up straight so that you can produce your voice without tension. Nothing is as detrimental to good voice quality as sitting round-shouldered in front of your computer or compressing your throat while you're on the phone.

3. **Headset:** Consider using a headset. When I'm talking to clients, reporters, or giving radio interviews, I always use a headset-and-microphone set-up. Doing so frees my body language, which listeners can hear in my voice. And yes, use a headset even for that brief outgoing message.

4. **Take some notes:** In both your outgoing message and those you leave when you make a call, take a moment to write down some key words concerning what you want to say. Don't create a script, though. The more you write, the more you'll read—so don't give yourself that temptation.

5. **Listen for vocal fillers.** You know these pests: "um," "uh," "er," "like," "you know," "right," "okay," and others. When listeners can't see anything, they're especially attuned to what your voice is doing. Just take your time with what you're saying, and get comfortable with silence!

6. **Watch out for "up-speak"!** Like, this is when everything you say sounds like a question? It can be, you know, really noticeable? If you want everything you say to sound tentative like that, use this form of speech. Otherwise, record yourself and develop the sound of assuredness.

78: Etiquette and Tactics for Conference Calls

If your workweek includes a fair amount of conference calls, you'll do well to keep the following tips in mind. You can file them under the heading "Phone Etiquette and Tactics."

To begin with, responsible phone behavior means not keeping your listeners in a state of confusion. You've probably found yourself in that position if you're talking to more than one person in a conference call and you're not sure whom *this* is, talking *now*. If you've never met the people before (a common situation), you may be at a total loss to know who's speaking since you can't recognize their individual voice. "Was that Pamela?" you'll find yourself saying. So when it's your turn to talk in a group call, identify yourself before you say something.

When your team is on a call together, consider whether you're creating a balance of "voice time." The same people who monopolize meetings may do it on conference calls! Also, if you don't speak much during a call, you're basically invisible. When you meet face-to-face later with the other group, they may have no idea who you are.

Give some thought to the placement of the phone on your end and the seating arrangements. Phones in speaker mode can degrade voice quality dramatically, so everyone sounds like they're at the bottom of a barrel. And people sitting too far away from the phone will sound like they're in the hallway.

And those conference calls where you have to punch in a code? Once you do, remember to announce that you've just joined the call. If you hear silence, speak up every fifteen or twenty seconds to remind anyone who may have just joined the call that you're already onboard. Otherwise, everyone may be sitting around in silence or chatting with the other people on their end of the line, with no one aware that all hands are now on deck.

79: How to Leave a Voice Message

Consider for a moment how many customers, clients, prospects, and stakeholders experience you through an outgoing or incoming voice message before ever getting to meet you in person. Ask yourself how many doors a professional-sounding message may open for you… or keep closed.

Here are just a few of the variables people may equate with you, merely from the sound of your phone messages:

- Confidence
- Control
- Friendliness
- Competence
- Intelligence
- Experience
- Warmth
- Calmness
- Empathy
- Stress level
- Openness
- Conciseness
- Clarity of thought
- Approachability
- Leadership
- Urgency
- Sense of humor
- Anger
- Professionalism

Now ask yourself if the phone messages you're creating give the impression you want to convey. Do you even listen to your outgoing message to get a sense of what others are hearing? If not, you need to! You can also practice leaving messages on your own business line to see how you're doing with that end of the deal.

Apart from those important questions of whether your messages are clear, concise, and help create interest, here are three ways to improve the effectiveness of the "you" that others hear—and judge—solely via the phone:

1. State your name and telephone number S-L-O-W-L-Y: It's surprising how many people sprint through their name and phone number. Remember that your listener may not have heard either before. Why make anyone listen two or three times to your message while getting annoyed?

2. Take time with your company's name. Some years ago, I conducted training for a law firm. Naturally, there were four names consisting of ten syllables in the name of the firm. It was such common practice to fly through it all too fast, that everyone laughed when I mentioned that they were doing it.

3. Work on your flow. Conciseness is essential in voice messages, but so is the flow of what you're saying. Are the messages you leave choppy, with awkward pauses? Or does the point you're making flow smoothly while sounding brisk and professional? It's a synergy you should aim for!

Handling Q & A
Like A Pro

"The Hatter opened his eyes very wide on hearing this;
but all he said was, 'Why is a raven like a writing-desk?'

'I give it up,' Alice replied: 'What's the answer?'

'I haven't the slightest idea,' said the Hatter."

— LEWIS CARROLL

80: Q & A: The Forgotten Avenue to Audience Persuasion

What's your relationship with the question-and-answer session that typically follows a speech or presentation? Which of the following two main camps do you reside in?

Camp Concerned: *I feel confident in my talk itself. But I dread what follows since I can't anticipate the questions that will be coming my way!*

OR

Camp Calm: *I relish the opportunity to engage with the people in the room. Now at last we can have a real dialogue on the topic!*

Whichever of these two environs feels like home to you—or even if neither of them do—remember that question-and-answer sessions are golden opportunities for persuasion and influence.

That's because Q & A offers a platform for stating your message all over again while presenting you at your professional best. Anyone can give a good speech if they know their topic and have prepared sufficiently. But few speakers can handle the rough-and-tumble of audience reactions to their performance with consummate grace.

You need to be one of them.

To understand how even challenging Q & A sessions can work to your advantage, picture the following scenario:

You're an audience member who has just listened to an excellent presentation by an authority on this topic. Now the speaker announces that she'll take questions.

Usually, one of three things happens at this point (or they *all* happen):

1. An audience member asks a devilishly difficult and insightful question, one that's so good you wish you'd thought of it yourself.

2. Someone stands up and begins pontificating at such length that you find you're in painful sympathy with the speaker.

3. The person right behind you starts attacking the presenter in a personal and nasty manner, while you attempt to dematerialize out of sheer embarrassment.

How the speaker responds in each of these scenarios depends upon many factors. These include the topic and speaking situation, the speaker's reputation and personality, the make-up of the audience, the intimacy of the talk, and so on.

One fact remains constant, however: *the person who handles herself with professionalism and aplomb in each of these situations grows in stature and credibility with the entire audience.*

Q & A, in other words, offers a priceless opportunity for you to shine in ways that your presentation, where you basically interact with no one, doesn't.

Let's look at some of the specific opportunities afforded by the question-and-answer period:

- It allows you to strongly reinforce or amplify your message.

- It's your last chance to make a positive impression on your audience. This is especially important if you've encountered difficulties in your presentation itself.

- It allows you to provide essential information that a) wasn't included in your talk, or b) wasn't sufficiently clear to the audience. Remember, if one person doesn't understand something, many more audience members who couldn't summon the courage to ask the question in public are probably also confused.

- It gives you the opportunity to issue your "call to action."

So whether you're a Q & A lover or hater, remind yourself that the question-and-answer session isn't just the tail end of your presentation. It's a strategic tool to be used for further persuasion and influence.

81: What If Nobody's Asking Questions?

Ask any actor if they have a recurring nightmare and the answer will almost certainly be: "I dream that I'm on stage on opening night and I can't remember my lines."

Clichéd perhaps. But it's still enough to make any actor wake up in a cold sweat. I still get that one myself from time to time. Public speakers have their own nightmare, and it looks like this: "I finish my speech and start the Q & A... *and nobody asks a single question!*"

As it happens, the speaker's nightmare is worse than the actor's. Actors occasionally do forget their lines, of course. But it usually isn't for very long; and any competent actor will be able to recover in character without the audience being any the wiser. (Did you know that the best-trained performers are able to improvise in iambic pentameter if they forget their lines while performing Shakespeare?)

The actor's nightmare, then, stays mostly in the world of unpleasant nocturnal fantasies. Not so the public speaker's dilemma. We've all been in situations when no one volunteers a question after we've finished a speech. In fact, it's a common occurrence.

Here are four remedies for this situation that I know you too fear more than the return of the Bubonic Plague:

Solution #1: "Show and Tell." When you say, "Does anyone have any questions?" raise your own hand. This gives listeners permission to follow your lead. And anyway, it's a visual demonstration of the action you want to take place.

Solution #2: "The Salvage Operation." Bring up an earlier comment or question. You can say, for instance: "Well, in the earlier program, this gentleman asked whether…"

The salvaged question may be something you didn't have time to address previously. It might also be a comment you mentally saved in your favorites folder for just such an occurrence. So start listening closely to comments made by audience members either during your speech, while others are speaking, or during the coffee break. You may gather material you'll be able to use later in Q & A.

Solution #3: "Does anyone have any questions for my answers?" That line is one that Henry Kissinger actually used at a press conference. I think it's perfect for this strategy. Seize the moment (since apparently, no one else will) and ask your question yourself!

You might say something like: "Well, I'm often asked…" or "One of the things people wonder about this subject is…" Have at least a half-dozen of these home-baked questions ready to pop out of your presentation toaster when the time is right. Just remember that they should be used at intervals during Q & A, not one after the other.

Solution #4: "Desperate Times Require Desperate Measures."
Throw in an activity that involves everyone. Basically, anything is fair game as long as it doesn't appear to be punishment for not asking any questions!

You could say, for example: "Great! This gives us the opportunity to do something I was hoping we'd have time for. Everyone please turn to the person on your left..." and away you go.

Whichever of the above solutions you choose, it should be initiated speedily. Nothing is worse than a long painful pause, punctuated with remarks by the speaker such as, "C'mon, SOMEBODY has to have a question!"

The good thing about these remedies is that they will grease the wheels so that questions start rolling your way. And if not, that's okay, because I have this activity...

82: Four Reasons You Should Love Q & A Sessions

If you've read the previous two Quick Tips, you should at least be on speaking terms with question-and-answer sessions. You're now aware that Q & A is an excellent avenue of persuasion. And you know some techniques for starting the ball rolling with questions following your presentation.

Now I'd like to convince you of why you should look forward to the Q & A period because of the benefits it could bring to your speeches.

The greatest of these is that Q & A gives you the chance to enrich and deepen listeners' experience of your talk. That in itself should be refreshing for both you and your audience. Yet there are at least four more reasons why you should love Q & A. Here they are:

Reason #1: Your presentation may have confused some audience members or left them unconvinced. Or worse, left them

unimpressed with you as a speaker.

In such cases, Q & A is your golden opportunity to either continue to inform and convince—or to do so at last as you conclude your presentation. Remember that speakers who handle themselves with style and assuredness in the no-holds-barred ring of Q & A may win over some listeners for the first time!

Reason #2: It's your chance to clarify your argument, give examples of your solution in action, or overcome opposition.

Most of the time you're challenged as a speaker to get essential information into a too-brief presentation period. Because Q & A gives the appearance of being audience controlled rather than speaker controlled, it allows you to expand your argument while responding directly to listeners "off the clock." The atmosphere created should feel more relaxed while giving you greater scope to deepen your audience's understanding.

Reason #3: Q & A is more conversational and natural than a one-way speech.

All effective public speaking is *conversational*, since audiences want speakers to communicate with them honestly and openly in everyday language. Too often, speeches have the feel of a monologue delivered to a polite but anesthetized audience.

The back-and-forth of Q & A should feel more comfortable to you AND listeners. Best of all, when you're conversing about a topic you truly care about, all of your best qualities as a speaker emerge.

Reason #4: Q & A demands your absolute best.

Face it: Q & A is a tremendous challenge. You can practice your presentation to your heart's content, but you can't know the queries and objections that may be coming your way.

To excel in Q & A, you have to be 100% focused and able to think on your feet. You need to be sensitive to the audience's feelings and opinions. You should demonstrate empathy toward others' viewpoints and values. Oh, and you have to remain spontaneous, flexible, logical, and good-natured.

Accomplish all of this—with a sense of humor and self-depreccation thrown in—and you'll understand why you may surpass the effectiveness of your speech itself.

83: The 7 Danger Zones of Q & A

Earlier in this chapter, I said that Q & A is one of the most challenging aspects of public speaking. Yet it's also one of your greatest opportunities to shine as a presenter.

If you can field questions with panache, think on your feet, and marshal forms of evidence with only seconds' notice, you'll convince listeners that you're at the top of your game.

That's not to say that audiences—including journalists, if they happen to be present—will make it easy for you. In fact Q & A sessions tend to bring out the worst and sometimes the angriest of our critics. So prepare yourself beforehand for a few grenades that may be lobbed your way.

What follows in this Quick Tip is your own ammunition toolbox. It's part of the segment of my workshops that I call "The 7 Danger Zones of Q & A." It includes a brief explanation of the worst types of questions you will face in question-and-answer sessions, with comments about how you can best cope with each one.

"The 7 Danger Zones"

1. Hostile questions
2. Loaded questions
3. Leading questions
4. Hypothetical questions
5. Multifaceted questions
6. Fuzzy questions
7. False choices.

1. **Hostile Questions:** Hostile questions often reflect pent-up anger directed at you simply because you're a convenient target. *"I've been dealing with salespeople like you for thirty years, and I'm sick and tired of hearing..."* has very little to do with your personality or competence.

    The key to handling hostility from questioners is to stay in control emotionally, and to listen carefully to what is behind or underneath the question. (In the theater, we call this information the *subtext* to what is spoken aloud.) Try to grasp the emotional context or underlying problem and address yourself to that as much as possible.

    Remember also that responding to hostile questions means not losing sight of your objective in terms of *persuasion*. Your chief purpose is still to advance the goals of your presentation, not to respond to your opponents' artillery barrage with your own display of verbal pyrotechnics.

2. **Loaded Questions:** These interrogatory packages are just what they sound like: explosive. And as the speaker, you are being invited to light the fuse! Since loaded questions are filled with damaging assumptions and conclusions, your job is similar to that of the Bomb Squad: to defuse the charge and bring the situation under control.

    Most important in doing so, *you must recast the assumption that is harming your case into more constructive language.* "Well, I can't agree with your interpretation that..." or "First, I have to correct something that you just said," are two options you can use, or similar phrasing.

    An important rule: The more damaging the assumption voiced by the questioner (that the entire audience hears, after all), the quicker you must refute it. If that means interrupting the questioner in the middle of the question-but-really-an-attack, go right ahead.

3. **Leading Questions:** A leading question is one in which the

preferred answer is embedded in the question itself. "Isn't it true that… ?" is a classic opening to a leading question, since the questioner obviously believes that "it" is true.

This is a sweet deal for the questioner, since it involves simultaneously asking the question and answering it in the way that reinforces his or her viewpoint! But you mustn't let that happen. Listen carefully so that you can hear when the person has slipped in a damaging assumption. That's the time to recast any such assertion (see point #2, above).

4. **Hypothetical Questions:** These are really "swamp" questions since they will lead you into a bog you may not find your way out of. Why go there at all?

A simple standard response of, "I can't answer a hypothetical situation like that" should suffice. The one exception is to go ahead and answer if your response to the hypothetical question makes a point you'd like to be heard.

For instance, when national security advisor Condoleezza Rice said that President George W. Bush's administration would consider it "a grave threat" if North Korea tested a nuclear device, she obviously intended to send a political message. As you can imagine, diplomats and negotiators are very skilled about using this option to respond to hypotheticals.

5. **Multifaceted Questions:** This too-many-bites-at-the-apple transgression appears frequently, particularly among journalists. The challenge here is that the many facets of the question(s), or the sheer length of the diatribe which precedes the actual question (if there is one) can make these interrogatories a real nuisance. Even that last sentence tested your patience didn't it?

Multifaceted questions can work to your advantage, however. That's because they allow you to answer as many of the facets as you like while ignoring the rest. If the question is long enough or convoluted, the audience probably won't notice what you've left out!

You can also take advantage of a multifaceted question by going directly to your main talking points, thereby restating your critical message. Again, the questioner has opened the door for you by behaving unreasonably and impractically.

6. **Fuzzy Questions:** This one is an All-Time-Greatest-Hits candidate for TV interviews and radio call-in shows. When a questioner's thinking is as sharp as the surface of a tennis ball, you should basically say a silent thank-you, and take your answer in any direction you like. You may also ask for a more targeted question from that person, but why give up the chance to state your message all over again?

7. **False Choices:** A false choice is an example of a *fallacy*, or an error in reasoning. E.g., "Look, we've got to use the budget surplus for either new bleachers in the gym or repaving the parking lot. Those are the things the school needs, and we can't afford both. So let's make up our minds!"

Why are those the only two choices? In reality, there are probably a dozen options in such a situation. When someone offers you a false choice, simply point out that there are, in fact, other alternatives then begin to discuss your favorites.

84: How to Tackle a Question-Hog

You know that person who monopolizes your time during Q & A, asking follow-up after follow-up to his original question? How about the pontificator who gives a lengthy treatise *as an introduction* to the question she eventually asks? Or the person who's more interested in broadcasting the depth of his knowledge than actually inquiring about anything?

These people are question-hogs.

As a speaker you have to keep these critters in their pen where they belong. The way you do it is by exercising control.

Question-hogs aren't just a Q & A nuisance—they have the potential to disrupt the entire time management of your question-and-answer session. They keep you from building momentum or flow. They put fellow audience members into an irreversible coma. And they vote the wrong way in every single election!

We can agree then that you have to stop question-hogs whenever they start to stampede. You therefore have permission to use the ultimate weapon:

Eye contact.

Here's how it works: When a question-hog asks a question, you begin your response while looking directly at the questioner. Very soon, however, you "open up" your answer to the entire barnya—er, audience. Now you're looking at everyone except the questioner. Most important, that's where you conclude your answer.

You thus have plausible deniability concerning the person who's waving an arm frantically in the air, i.e., the question-hog. You're looking at the other side of the room by now, so YOU DON'T EVEN SEE HIM!

Of course, you do notice the hand of the polite audience member on that side of the room who's been patiently waiting for her turn.

You see, despite what your spouse believes, a roving eye is a good thing.

Just don't tell said spouse I told you that.

85: Emerging from Q & A as a Winner

Here's a way to conclude your Q & A sessions dynamically and convincingly. It generally will boost your credibility with audiences; and best of all it's simple to remember.

In fact, it's as easy as "1-2-3."

That's because you never say: "We have time for *one* [or *two* or *three*] more question(s)."

You avoid completely being that dangerously specific. Here's why:

What if the last question (after you said, "We have time for one more") is a nightmare, involving a dilemma Solomon himself couldn't untangle? Is that the way you want to end your make-or-break presentation?

The "Two Questions" Mistake: Suppose you're giving a sales talk, and Questioner #2 (since you invited "Two more questions") takes the opportunity to accuse your company of turning out overpriced junk for the past 20 years?

The "Three Questions" No-No: What if the final contribution from the audience (Hey, you *did* say, "We can take three more questions") reveals the single weakness in your argument that you were really, really hoping you wouldn't be asked about?

You see the point.

Now for the simple solution:

Instead of falling into the "one, two, or three more" trap, you say, "We have time for a *few more* questions."

So how many is that anyway? Two, three, four, five? *I* don't know!

In other words, you end the Q & A whenever you like. If it happens to be just after a response that concludes your talk in a blaze of glory, well, that's just the way it happened.

Isn't it?

86: I Hope You Never Get Asked a Question Like This One

It was an appearance on live radio in which I was being interviewed about my second book, *Fearless Speaking*. The program was a business radio show, and per the usual procedure I was given the starting time, the length of the show, and the name of the host. I was to call into the show ten minutes before we were scheduled to go on the air and check in with the producer.

That's when the producer said, "Thanks so much, Dr. Genard, for agreeing to talk to our panel."

"Did you say *panel?*"

"Yes, this is our business roundtable, and you'll be talking to four local business owners."

Well, that was fine, I thought. The topic—how to overcome fear of public speaking—was appropriate for employees or business owners themselves who have to make pitches and presentations. Ten minutes later, we went on the air. And this is what the host said to me after he'd introduced me to the panelists:

"Dr. Genard, we ask the same question of all our guests on this show: If you died and went to heaven, what song would you sing to be allowed inside?"

Yes, I did say this was *live radio.*

Now, it didn't matter that this question had absolutely nothing to do with the topic of my book, or that no one gave me a heads-up beforehand that this from-the-planet-Pluto question would be asked. The only thing that did matter, was that I was just asked it, and I had better come up with a reply fast.

So I said, "*God Bless America?*"

Oh, no, the panel snorted: that was too easy! "Come up with something else, please." And I did:

"How about the old Hoagy Carmichael song, *Stardust?*" I said. "The music has a mysterious heavenly quality to it, and I've always loved that song."

"Dr. Genard says *Stardust!*" the host proclaimed.

The panel thought that was just fine. But the host wasn't finished.

"You're an actor and a singer, right?" he said to me. "Can you sing some of the song for us?"

Well, believe it or not, I knew I was on solid ground now, as singing on the air didn't bother me at all. So I did, the panel and host applauded, and we got on with the interview.

The point I want to make to you isn't, start memorizing a heavenly song because you never know when you'll be asked for one in a radio interview. It's that Q & A is totally unpredictable, and you truly never know what may be headed your way. Equally important: *you can't prepare for what you don't know is coming.*

The key is, knowing your topic, and having faith in yourself that you'll come up with something appropriate and professional. That day on the radio, I had a truly bad couple of seconds when I thought, "I can't possibly answer that question, I'm supposed to be good at this and here I am dying right here on the air!" But that's all it was: a couple of seconds; then my brain did the processing it needed to do when I needed that to happen.

The same process will more than likely happen for you too when you need it. And if you're asked something so far out of left field that you can't possibly answer it—and shouldn't be expected to—you can always say, "Well, what I'm really here to talk about is [your topic]."

Incidentally, at the end of the 45-minute show, the host said, "Dr. Genard, we have a surprise for you. Our engineer has found Nat King Cole's recording of *Stardust*. We'd like to play it for you."

And they did. As we all listened to Nat Cole's famous rendition of the song, one of the panelists said:

"Nat King Cole sounds just like Dr. Genard!"

Bless her heart.

Nuts & Bolts:
Practical Skills for Presenters

"Keep your eyes on the stars, and your feet on the ground."

—THEODORE ROOSEVELT

87: Food, Caffeine, and Energy

What's your drug of choice as a speaker?

Is it coffee?

Some pre-speech cans of Coke?

A mind-numbing martini or three?

If you're looking for focus, dynamism, and power as a speaker, your primary energy source should be *proper breathing*, rather than any of the usual suspects named above. That, along with solid preparation and practice, will bring you more reliably to the peak of performance concerning sufficiently energized speaking.

Breathing creates the energy that powers the vibration of your vocal cords, projecting the sound outward to listeners. But what about the rest of your physical performance as a presenter? What can give you enough of a boost to make you lively and animated from your first word to your last?

The answer is carbohydrates and caffeine.

Both play a role in energizing your presentation persona.

Carbohydrates. If you're a devotee of a low-carbohydrate or no-carbohydrate diet, you're putting yourself at an energy disadvantage as a public speaker. Protein is the building block of new tissue, but it doesn't provide a reliable and predictable source of energy the way carbohydrates do.

Here's how your body's energy-producing factory works: What ultimately gives you energy as a speaker, aside from your passion for your topic, is sugar. This is good news—at least for non-diabetics—since it is easy to control the level of sugar in your bloodstream.

Simple sugars such as refined sugar, orange juice, candy, etc., produce energy immediately. And *complex carbohydrates* such as pasta, bread, etc., turn into sugar gradually as your body processes them.

By taking in a combination of simple sugars and complex carbohydrates, you can provide yourself with an energy supply that is sustained for the entirety of your presentation. The orange juice and the sugar in your tea at breakfast gave you an immediate boost; and the toast or pastries you also had will provide an ongoing energy supply for the next two to three hours.

Be aware, however, that fat-laden sugary foods such as chocolate bars and other rich confections can slow you down, since your body processes fats very slowly.

Caffeine. If you also depend upon caffeine to provide your oomph factor, know that a time lag operates between the ingestion of your beverage of choice and its energy benefits. Depending on your personal metabolism, caffeine may reach its full effect only after an hour or more. And it may continue to perform its magic for up to four hours after ingestion. [1]

So if you were up all night preparing and you're depending upon that gallon of coffee to pry your eyes open, keep this relatively long lead-time in mind.

---

[1] Baker and Theologus 1972, quoted in Anthony P. Winston, Elizabeth Hardwick, and Neema Jaberi, "neuro-psychiatric effects of caffeine," Advances in Psychiatric Treatment 2005 (vol. 11, 433). Accessed January 22, 2007 at http://apt.rcpsych.org/cgi/reprint/11/6/432.pdf.

If on the other hand caffeine turns you into Mr. or Ms. Hyde, time your last injection so that it will *wear off* before you get up to speak.

All systems go, then?

"10… 9… 8… 7… 6…"

88: How to Speak from Notes or a Manuscript

It isn't difficult to read from notes or a manuscript in a speech while still relating to your listeners.

Why then do so many people do it badly? It can't be because speakers find it fruitful to pretend there's no one actually listening to their speeches. And it can't possibly help to have a closer relationship with your notes than with your audience.

After all, if the whole idea behind a presentation is to influence listeners, a speaker had better find a way to establish rapport with the audience! Are *you* willing to be influenced by someone who basically denies your existence?

What follows are six practical tips for remaining effective when speaking from a manuscript or notes. These suggestions will help you remain engaging and influential as a speaker while maintaining a conversational dynamic with listeners.

1. **Write to speak.** Compose your talk for the *ears* of listeners, not their *eyes*. After all, they don't see your text! Also, aim for a conversational rhythm rather than the more formal style of memos and reports (or the sloppy syntax of email messages). That means using simple words and short sentences, creating word pictures, and telling stories.

2. **Make it easy for you to read.** Give yourself pages that you can read easily from the lectern. Use a large typeface, triple margins, and avoid the bottom of the page so your audience isn't looking at the top of your head.

3. **Grab key phrases and run with them.** You don't want to spend more performance time with your text than with listeners. So look down and "grab" key phrases and sentences. Then look up at your audience and say them. Practice the technique to acquire a rhythm, for this is an essential speaker's skill. An important general rule: *If you're not looking at your audience, nothing should be coming out of your mouth.*

4. **Use the pause that refreshes.** That's an old ad slogan, but it applies to public speakers that must learn to use pauses. Pauses help shape your speech. They show that you're confident enough to let an idea sink in. They're refreshing for listeners. Adrenalin will try to make you speed up, but you must take time to pause. A speech without pauses seems to go on forever, regardless of its actual length.

5. **Look at the listeners.** This is the forest that speakers don't see because the trees that make up the pages of their manuscript are getting in the way. You must look up from your speech with every sentence you utter. We audience members need eye contact to believe you're talking to us; and if you won't look us in the eye, you simply won't persuade us.

6. **Hit your peaks.** Remember that your speech or presentation needs shape, in terms of both ideas and vocal delivery. A speech lacking a climax, for instance, is as formless as an amoeba; and presentations without vocal variety are dreary affairs. The tendency of your voice to "flatten out" increases when you read from notes or a manuscript instead of conversing with listeners. Remind yourself in every instance that you are talking to people not sheets of paper. People demand much more from you than lifeless words on a page. But if you breathe life into those words, listeners will return the favor handsomely.

89: Surviving an Encounter with a Wild Lectern

If you've read this far in this book, chances are you're aware that speaking in public can be exhilarating and rewarding. In fact, delivering a key speech or presentation can be career enhancing in ways that few endeavors are.

There's another side to public speaking, however. The dark truth is that there are speech-related objects and props that will eat you alive if given half a chance.

Note cards, projectors, laptops, and microphones all fall into this category. But for sheer aggression and potential for lasting damage, nothing beats the lectern.

The lectern! The very symbol of public humiliation and thwarted ambitions! Rapport-destroying barricade! (And don't be fooled by its tendency to masquerade as a "podium," or the harmless platform you stand on when you speak.)

No, lecterns are those big blocky monsters that prevent access to listeners, and vice-versa. Worse, *they love to gobble speakers whole!*

But do not despair. Here are 5 essential rules of survival you can follow if you find yourself locked in mortal combat with one of these voracious predators.

Survival Rule #1: Keep both feet planted firmly on the floor, even if your audience can't see them. If you lean on one leg—or worse, cross your feet—you will look and feel unstable. That's bad enough. But lecterns have been known to bite off the appendages of speakers who leave a foot or leg off on its own.

Survival Rule #2: Gesture frequently with your hands and arms *so the lectern doesn't realize you're frozen with fear.* If you remain perfectly still, a mature lectern will either a) think you are made of wood like it is and attempt to absorb you completely; or b) realize that you are paralyzed by fear and therefore unable to defend yourself. It will then immediately initiate hostile actions.

Survival Rule #3: If you make the unwise choice to keep your arms totally still, at least *place one hand lightly on either side of your manuscript.* Don't let your hands disappear completely from view (see Rule #1 about vulnerable appendages). Leaning heavily on the lectern itself, on the other hand, will make you appear truculent or drunk, and the added pressure will make the lectern very angry.

Survival Rule #4: DO NOT GRASP THE FRONT OR SIDES OF A LECTERN WITH A GRIP THAT REMOVES THE BLOOD FROM YOUR FINGERS. White knuckles are a particular delicacy for lecterns.

Survival Rule #5: Step away from the lectern occasionally if the speech situation allows it, i.e., if your nose is not attached to your manuscript. This will strengthen your engagement with the audience, and eliminate the physical barrier between you and them. But much more importantly, you'll have a head start of a step or two if those jaws open wiiiiiide!

90: How Video Can Transform Your Public Speaking

I'd like to tell you about an amazing testament to the power of videotaping in public speaking training. And this result came about when I least expected it.

As an actor and speech coach, I use video constantly to help my clients achieve stage presence and a powerful performance persona. So I'm used to hearing people say they dread seeing themselves, yet adding after they do, "It wasn't as bad as I thought!"

But that day in our training room was different. My client was a father of the bride preparing for the traditional wedding reception toast. He was excited and apprehensive and wanted to help make the day special for the newlyweds, just like any member of a wedding party.

The fact that he had a neurological condition that affected his speech hadn't made a huge impression on me. After all, he faced the same need everyone does who delivers a speech at a wedding, funeral, or special event: to speak to the best of his or her ability and reflect well on the occasion. Audiences at these events *always* care more about true feeling than they do slickness in a presenter. So I was working with him on honestly and simply conveying what he was feeling.

But his reaction on seeing himself on video caught me completely off guard. His medical condition makes his gaze wander constantly, and causes his head to jerk slightly from time to time. When he saw this on video, he was profoundly disturbed. I told him not to worry, since he couldn't do anything about his condition and most of his audience was aware of it. But he said he would do something—he would concentrate on staying still and making his eye contact steady, through sheer self-control, for the entire five minutes of his toast.

And he did it! It really was an extraordinary demonstration of the power of concentration in a speaker. Equally important, it brought home to me as dramatically as possible just how valuable a video camera can be in preparing for a public speaking appearance. Below are four more reasons why videotaping your own practice sessions is a great idea.

Video Reveals Your Energy Level as a Speaker. Isaac Newton said that, "For every action, there's an equal and opposite reaction." Give your audience an energetic performance and they in turn will respond more enthusiastically. Video will help you see where you fall on the speaker's energy meter.

Video Can Help You Stay More Focused. "I look like I'm following a mouse with my eyes!" my client said as he watched his statement on video. The client happened to be a United States Senator, and our coaching session was taking place in the Capitol building in Washington. His staff and I laughed at the Senator's humorous remark about his appearance in the Congressional hearing and then we got down to business. Over the next two hours, the video camera helped him develop the ability to look at his listeners with unwavering attention. A couple of years later, when I saw him in an election ad on TV, I was amazed at how much he'd improved in his ability to stay focused in front of a television camera.

Video Puts Your Body Language Front-and-Center. "I wander back and forth constantly." "I seem to be swaying in an invisible breeze." "I'm listing to starboard!" Clients sometimes react with comments like these when seeing themselves on video. There's no doubt about it: video reveals how nonverbal communication can trump anything you say. When you realize that you have a habit of rubbing your belly when speaking (as one of my clients saw herself doing), you'll appreciate this tool for experiencing yourself the way others do.

Video Can Boost Your Confidence. Given some of those examples above, you may be skeptical when I say that videotaped practice is a confidence booster. Sure, it may show you some things that will horrify you. But awareness is the first step to changing counterproductive behavior. (And there's always that common "It's not as bad as I thought!" reaction as well.)

Then there's the Before-and-After Effect. The amount of your own improvement as a speaker can be hard to quantify at times; but there's no mistaking the progress you've made when you see it revealed on tape.

So start using that video camera, smartphone, or tablet. When you see and hear how far you've come, you may have the same response many of my clients do:

"Wow."

91: Jokes, Humor, and Other Serious Stuff

I don't know whether the chicken or the egg came first. But I *do* know the question that preceded both:

"Should I start my speech with a joke?"

Well, in fowl weather or fair, it all depends.

Humor entertains, of course; and it can be a tool of persuasiveness in public speaking. But unless people laugh good-naturedly whenever you walk into a room, you shouldn't give humor the central role in your talk. That advice holds even for after-dinner speeches, which are supposed to be entertaining. Any humor in your speeches still has to serve the message you're imparting, just like every other element of your talk.

So let's look at how humor can help you achieve speaking success, as well as the places where the ice gets a bit thin.

Jeff Fleming said this in the pages of *Professional Speaker*, the journal of the National Speakers Association: "Humor makes an audience more receptive to your message, improves retention of points made, reduces tension, improves creativity and provides entertainment value to any presentation." [2]

Pretty effective stuff, humor! We might also add that humor allows an audience to see that you're human and to identify with you. And it lets everybody in the room have some fun.

Like any presentation tool, however, humor must be used judiciously and in the context of your message. Here's an example of what happens when those two considerations *aren't* taken into account:

Some years ago, I conducted a workshop at a large multinational manufacturing firm. Vice presidents from fully a dozen departments were represented, from finance to distribution. On the workshop's second day, each participant had to give a 10-minute

---

[2] Jeff Fleming, "Observational Humor: Seeing What Others Are Thinking," *Professional Speaker,* November 2005, 10.

presentation that we videotaped and discussed afterwards. One of the executives started his speech with a joke. Now, this was a stretch-limo of a joke that ate up the first 3 ½ minutes of his allotted ten minutes. Even worse, it was about the *Pope*!

How's that for living dangerously?

This brief true story contains four valuable lessons about how to use humor in presentations:

1. The humor shouldn't take up so much time that it competes with the body of your presentation.

2. The humor should be culturally appropriate. In other words, you should have a reasonable idea of whether it's safe to use. Who knows, for instance, how many Catholics would be in this executive's future audiences and would be offended by a joke about the Pope?

3. The humor must be *closely related* to your topic. In the above case, the presenter labored mightily to tie his punch line with the topic that followed, but it was an impossible task.

4. Using humor is usually productive, while *telling a joke* is inviting T-R-O-U-B-L-E. There's a world of difference, that is, between relating a humorous story an audience can relate to, and handing them a zinger of a sidesplitting gag—and hoping that they'll laugh.

   Telling a joke well requires timing, the ability to assume voices and characterizations, and the honed skills of a stand-up comic. These needs are usually worlds apart from the credibility you must achieve with business and professional audiences.

   So keep it safe and in good taste—just like the products from the Good Humor Man.

92: When Your Audience Has Eaten a Bowling Ball for Lunch

Unless you have a death wish, I suggest you object to giving your presentation immediately after lunch. This slot is second only in the Presentation Horrors Hall of Fame to being the speaker just *before* lunch.

The world of business speeches and presentations being what it is, however, there will be times when you're asked to speak in either of these situations. My advice for the before-lunch slot is simple and straightforward: shorten your presentation by one-third. This will keep you from being the entrée, and you may even get an extra slice of dessert for your niceness.

My advice for the post-prandial presentation requires more discussion.

So, what can you do when each audience member's blood supply has fled from brain to belly to handle the all-too-common conference meal of beef or seafood, rich mashed potatoes, buttery green beans, cheesecake, and coffee-with-cream? (I'm assuming, of course, that you yourself have dined lightly on carbohydrates to provide you with a continuing source of energy over the next couple of hours. Right?)

In such dire circumstances, you must think *activity*.

This encompasses a wide continuum that includes everything from stimulating creative thinking, to getting your audience on its feet for calisthenics. And I'm not kidding! I routinely have C-suite executives and U.N. ambassadors performing jumping jacks.

The one thing you don't want your audience to be allowed to do is to settle comfortably in their seats while your PowerPoint presentation weighs heavily on everyone's eyelids.

Instead, let your audience know that it's NOT SAFE when you're in the room. Insist on participation—mental or physical or both—right from the start of your talk. Pose a question as early as you can: not a rhetorical question but one that demands an answer. (If you don't know enough about this audience to do that intelligently, start doing your research!)

You might ask everyone to interact with the person next to him or her (e.g., "Introduce yourself and tell that person what your job is within the company" still works if you make it sound like fun). Or break listeners up into groups. That's right: you can do so even this early in your presentation.

Distribute a survey. Ask for a volunteer to demonstrate something. (Believe me, seeing your gaze travel over the audience when you say, "volunteer" will keep listeners attentive!) Or just get them on their feet for a good stretch. That one works just as well in an auditorium filled with people. Even simple techniques can be effective when everybody is fighting off the drowsies.

Remember, your presentation should always be about engaging audiences in every way possible. That objective just needs a little extra help when bowling ball tartare is on the menu.

93: Three Important Steps in Preparing and Practicing a Talk

Now that you've followed all the other advice in this book, you're ready to gather up your materials and give a dynamic and influential presentation. It should be an enjoyable experience for you and your audience.

And if the stars align—it could be a turning point in your career or your organization's success.

But like all great things, the nuts-and-bolts preparation you do beforehand is what will ensure your eventual success. In that spirit, here are three pieces of practical advice for "getting ready" with your speech, presentation, pitch, lecture, demonstration, or talk.

There's one bit of wisdom I'd like to share with you first, though. It's the best advice I know of for becoming a more accomplished presenter:

Acquire as much speaking experience as possible.

Take every opportunity to speak in public—even if that's a nerve-racking proposition for you. It's the best way to gain control over your fear, and to reach that state of mind in which speaking in front of others is both a pleasurable and productive activity for you.

Now, the practical advice:

1. **Prepare solid briefing materials.** Take a page from diplomats and other public affairs types and put together a briefing book. Ask yourself these questions as you compile your information:

   - Are my materials memorable (for *me*)?

   - Have I anticipated questions and objections?

   - Does each of my main points "headline" the information to come?

   - Is my information well laid out and visually highlighted for my benefit?

2. **Plan your practice sessions.** A good strategy for your practice sessions can be just as helpful as visualizing success in your presentation itself. Here's how to go about it:

   - **Timing:** Begin sooner rather than later. Give yourself sufficient time!

   - **Emphasis:** Be clear on what you're focusing on. For instance, are you looking for feedback on your content? Logic and language? Level of audience interaction? Visual components?

   - **Setting:** Go from rough-and-ready settings to as close an approximation as you can of the real situation, venue, and audience.

   - **Post-performance feedback:** Define for yourself what you'll consider a success, and let subordinates and colleagues know that you expect and welcome criticism.

- **Rehearse 3-5 times:** Less than three times is almost winging it. If you rehearse more than 5 times, you'll run the risk of a) becoming stale, and b) memorizing movements and repeating them so that they look mechanical.

3. **Have an out-of-body-experience.** Videotape yourself, or use a tape recorder if you'll be speaking on radio, a podcast, or a webinar. Watch, listen, and work on the rough spots. It's as simple as that.

You need to hear and see yourself as others experience you. The modern miracle of digital equipment allows you to do that. Make use of it!

94: A Checklist of Nonverbal Delivery Skills

Body Language: "Was my body language effective?"
- Did I demonstrate a confident yet relaxed posture?
- Did I include natural-looking movement while avoiding repetitive gestures?
- Were my gestures supportive of what I was saying?
- Was my face expressive of my ideas and emotions?
- Did I make direct and ongoing eye contact?

Vocal Qualities: "Was my voice interesting and dynamic?"
- Did I vary my pitch and speak at a reasonable tempo?
- Was my vocal tone pleasant and confident-sounding?
- Did I sound intellectually and emotionally committed to my ideas?
- Was my voice lively and energetic?
- Did I use pauses to let my important points sink in?

Use of Space: "Did I command the stage on which I spoke?"

- Did I "own" my space, not diminishing or over-expanding my physical presence?

- Was my movement fluid rather than abrupt or jerky?

- Did I sit or stand poised and ready, without slouching?

- Was I open (and not closed-off) physically?

- Was I animated instead of being stiff and wooden?

95: Lies, Damn Lies, and Statistics

"Father, I cannot tell a lie: Here in the Colonies, fully 37.8% of boys cut down a cherry tree as a normal part of adolescent development."

—WHAT GEORGE WASHINGTON REALLY SAID

Among the educational gems I remember from high school is one from Mr. McDevitt's 10th grade Economics class. He warned us to be careful of statistics. The exact same data, he told us, could be used to justify any position—including those that are directly opposed to each other.

I can certainly think of a political position or two that validate Mr. McDevitt's argument.

Mark Twain said all of this in another way. As he wrote in his *Autobiography* (attributing the remark to Benjamin Disraeli): "There are three kinds of lies—Lies, damn lies, and statistics."

For your purposes as a speaker, you must bear in mind yet another characteristic of these examples of numerical evidence: by themselves, statistics are cold, hard things. For audiences to relate to your statistics and take them to heart, you must humanize them.

Put another way, people will generally only remember a statistic if it is attached to human experiences and emotions, especially their own.

Let's take an example: Suppose you're giving a talk with an anti-smoking message. You could simply say, "Smoking-related diseases claim an estimated 440,000 American lives each year," [3] and leave it at that.

Or you could start out the same way, but add something more: "Smoking-related diseases claim an estimated 440,000 American lives each year. That's a big number, but what does it mean in terms of a scale we can understand? Well, it's the equivalent of a fully-loaded 757 airliner crashing, with everyone aboard killed, every day for *884 consecutive days, or two-and-a-half years.*"

Which version do you think would have more impact?

Another way to make your statistic vivid in listeners' minds is to bring it from the macro level to the micro level. Here, you frame the overwhelming statistic in terms of a single life. To stay with our health theme, for example: Suppose your message is how thousands of women who die each year could be saved by monthly breast self-examinations.

Rather than just tossing out your statistic, you could start out with the story of a single woman. After your greeting, for instance, you might say: "On September 8, 2009, Melissa Dougherty, a 31-year-old mother of two, noticed a tiny hard spot in her left breast. It was so small, and she was so young, she didn't think too much of it. The truth is, she was also a little scared. Six months went by as Melissa ignored the spot, until finally her husband noticed what had now unmistakably become a lump. It was Jack who convinced Melissa to have it checked out."

From that starting point, you begin to tell us of the ordeal Melissa faced as she was diagnosed with invasive ductal carcinoma and had to undergo surgery, radiation, and chemotherapy. That leads you into your message of why monthly breast self-examinations can be critical to saving women's lives (and your big statistic, if you have one, comes somewhere in there).

---

[3] http:/www.lungusa.org/site/pp.asp?c=dvLUK9O0E&b=39853, March 9, 2006.

Of course, with a strategy like this one, you must let your audience know what happened to "Melissa Dougherty." That is, you carefully didn't resolve the true story for your audience; instead keeping them interested in the woman you've introduced them to. Only at the end do you reveal that Melissa was lucky—as you tell listeners how regular breast self-examinations can keep more women from finding herself in her situation.

96: Seven Tips for a Successful Job Interview

As you know, or should know, a successful job search is only partly about the interview itself. Other behaviors that you exhibit are also important. These include your phone skills in setting up the interview, your prompt and professional follow-up to the meeting, any personal connections that can bolster your candidacy, and so on.

That said, your interaction with your interviewer(s) remains the single most important factor in landing a job. Here are seven suggestions for standing out from the crowd as you seek that dream job:

1. **Show confidence.** Your interviewers have brought you in because they genuinely want to know who you are and how you might fit into their organization. They'll have a hard time figuring any of this out if you sit blandly, responding robot-like to their questions.

   Have the confidence and courage to be you. That means taking your responses into your home territory, not merely following the crumbs to where you think they want you to go. Your interviewers know you're probably nervous. Exhibiting sufficient self-esteem will differentiate you from all the other candidates who come across as *just* nervous.

2. **Initiate.** When you walk into your interviewer's office, be the one to initiate the moment of greeting. "So nice to meet you.

Thank you for having me here today," is a simple yet great opener. Showing enough initiative to reach out first is a very good sign. So, act rather than react.

3. **Notice, and comment.** What is there in the room or situation that you can comment on? Do you have a mutual acquaintance or hobby? Is the view from the window stunning? What about that intriguing Balinese mask on the wall?

Remember, most applicants arrive, sit down, and begin taking questions. What's memorable about that? If you make an intelligent and appropriate comment to start out, you'll be remembered. Now take a seat once you're invited to, and keep in mind the following points as you speak:

4. **Organization and logic.** Show that you've invested some thought in this industry, company, and your possible place in the scheme of things. Try to make it appear that you're a self-starter with a nimble mind.

Make your points concisely and back them up with evidence. Be firm without being dogmatic, generous when mentioning others, personable but not silly. Impress them with the value of your opinions, without seeming to consider them worthy of Fort Knox.

5. **Enthusiasm.** Convey the impression that this employment opportunity excites you. Project enough energy that the interviewers pick up on it and get a charge themselves. They'll feel good about the interview afterwards, even if they can't put their finger on exactly why.

6. **Emotion (be human).** Don't buy into the myth that emotions have no place in the world of business and the professions. Be passionate about the things that matter to you (but don't come across as obsessive). Just be sure that your deeply held convictions are in line with their thinking and business practices.

7. **Smile.** You probably smile too infrequently when you're under pressure. If this job interview appears to be making you work

like hell, it'll seem like hard work for your interviewer too. He or she may even get the impression that the thought of being part of this organization is too difficult an undertaking for you. Instead of leading them to such a grim conclusion, try to seem like a pleasant person to be around.

Most of all, don't be a mysterious personage that needs information coaxed out of him or her, grunt by inconclusive response. That works for Hollywood anti-heroes and comic book crime-fighters, but not for gainfully employed professionals.

97: Toasts, Awards and Other Special Occasions

Speeches on special occasions can provoke greater anxiety than everyday, business-related speaking assignments. Yet the truth is that a request to speak at these events is an honor. Your position, closeness to the people or events being feted, or your distinction in your field is responsible for your place of prominence on the occasion.

That special knowledge or experience is what you should draw upon as you prepare and deliver your special occasion speech.

Tell the stories that *these* listeners will find interesting. In particular, reveal your personal connection with the honoree(s). But most of all—be honest. What the audiences at these events want is sincerity, not polish.

When one of my relatives died in his early fifties, he left his mother and three siblings. At his wake, the family asked me to read the eulogy his brothers and sister had written, which would be delivered during the funeral mass at the church the next day. They thought I would do a good job of it because I'm an actor.

I told them I would be happy to do so if they really wanted me to. But I told them it would mean much more to everyone if one of them read the eulogy concerning their brother. Eventually, they agreed. And though the sibling who spoke the words wasn't a polished speaker, he tapped into bittersweet emotions for the relatives that I'd never have been able to reach.

When it comes to public speaking on special occasions, honesty trumps show business every time. It isn't the wisdom of the ages listeners are hoping for—it's *your thoughts and emotions on the occasion.* So be confident in your worth as a valued contributor and speak from the heart.

Here's some specific advice you might bear in mind for particular events:

- **The Toast**. Eloquence is expected here. That doesn't mean that you must suddenly become a Fifth Avenue sophisticate. If you stay simple and true, conveying your honest affection for the honoree(s), *you will be eloquent.* This is also an ideal place to use quotations, either from people known personally to listeners or famous persons. A word to the wise: beware of alcohol, which may be flowing freely by the time you stand up to speak.

- **The Roast.** Introduce yourself if everyone in the room doesn't already know you. A general rule of roasts is that the closer you are to the "roastee," the further in you can slip your blade—all in good fun, of course. Remember that self-deprecating humor is always welcome at a roast, since it shows that you can take it as well as dish it out.

- **Master or Mistress of Ceremonies.** Maintain a firm but light touch. Don't make the mistake of thinking that just because you've been invited to be the MC, this is about you. It isn't. Learn the names and titles of the people you're introducing and then let them do their own thing. Perhaps most important, speak beforehand with your host to see what he or she wants you to do. Then give exactly that, no more and no less. And be sure you know how you're expected to dress.

- **Blessing, Grace, or Benediction.** A successful blessing combines the true and eternal with the particular. Prayers and profound thoughts from the Bible, poetry, and the wisdom of other religions and cultures are always appropriate. Bear in mind that you can also go outside the expected sources if you find something appropriate and refreshing. A beautiful feature of a prayer, for instance, can be your own addition, something original that you've thought up for the occasion. That's a way to take the eternal and link it to the special occasion of the gathering

- **Acceptance Speech or Response to a Testimonial.** Here, less is definitely more. Nothing sours an audience's goodwill more quickly than a too-long or self-indulgent acceptance speech. Think Oscars, and you'll know exactly what I mean. So, humbly thank your sponsors, mention others as accomplished as you who didn't win the award (or those you work with that collectively deserve it as much as you), and make a graceful exit.

- **Eulogy.** The surprising truth about eulogies is that they don't have to be sad and somber set pieces. Eulogies represent a wonderful opportunity for all present to celebrate the life of the person, not just mourn their passing. Here again, heartfelt emotion is the key. I gave the eulogy at my mother's funeral, and I had to stop speaking more than once because emotion overtook me and closed my throat. But I simply paused each time, collected myself, and went on.

   If you deliver a eulogy, find a way to tap into the joy that this person's life made possible. In the movie *Mr. Saturday Night,* Billy Crystal's character—a professional comedian—gives a hilarious and bittersweet eulogy at his mother's funeral. The fact that everyone is laughing throughout his talk in no way diminishes the deep affection the survivors have, and are busy showing, for the deceased.

Looking Ahead:
The Future of Public Speaking

"We all live every day in virtual environments,
defined by our ideas."

—MICHAEL CRICHTON

98: Are You Ready for the Future of Business Communication?

Are you ready for the way business communication will be conducted from now on?

If you answered yes, you probably realize that video will be part of that future. And along with video, there's webinars, podcasts, and online learning. In other words, some form of virtual engagement will increasingly be part of your professional life. And that means learning the art of speaking virtually.

Which is to say, the future is already here, and as speakers we need to recognize that fact. Video in particular will be a key driver of personal and organizational success. Consider the following:

The average American adult spends an average of 19 hours per month viewing online videos. Sixty percent of videos viewed are consumer products videos. Fifty-two percent of people say those videos helped them make a decision. [1]

Are you ready to offer the "virtual you" that the people you communicate with are expecting?

If you're not convinced yet that video is in your future, consider this fact: *Videos are 53 times more likely to get indexed than text-only content.* (And you have to have a 'big pop' in the first 15 seconds, because that's when a significant drop-off in viewer interest occurs.) [2]

You can tap into the video universe in different ways: on your website, in your blog, on online video sites, through social media, email marketing, online advertising, and embedded in QR codes. If the performance skills you need for dynamic virtual performances aren't in your DNA, a good speech coach can help you acquire them. What matters most is that you get your mind in the right place. That means understanding that "tomorrow" is here today, and that speaking virtually is a central part of it.

99: Presentation Technology... Are You Using it Effectively?

I've seen the future of presentation technology—in a keynote presentation that made it come to life. It all happened recently in Boston.

It's a big deal. And that's partly because it deals with Big Data.

If you've been paying attention the last few years, you know about Big Data—large data sets that are being captured, analyzed, and used strategically across sectors. And if your sector happens to

---

[1] Presentation by Melissa Albano-Davis, "Video Marketing and Optimization," at Constant Contact event, "Get Social Media Savvy for 2014," Waltham, Mass., December 10, 2013.

[2] Albano-Davis, 2013.

be healthcare, you may know about connected health, a trend that uses technology and the data it generates to provide care remotely.

Sometimes that involves patients with chronic conditions taking measurements and reporting them to healthcare professionals who interpret the data. Other times, wearable devices are used to provide feedback on vital signs, physical performance, stress levels, the number of steps taken in a day, sleeping habits, and so on.

The keynote I attended recently at a healthcare conference combined these trends, along with the concept of a virtual coach, in an interesting and exciting way. We were taken through a "typical day" in the life of the speaker in 2021, or five years in the future. Throughout the speaker's presentation, the voice of the virtual coach would intervene (it was cleverly pre-recorded using the well-known voice of a local broadcaster). With reminders, cautions, suggestions, and even opportunities mentioned that coincided with the speaker's location at that moment, the coach kept the speaker in synch with his healthcare goals, *all because of the personal data the speaker's "wearables" were generating.*

As I watched this presentation, a question presented itself that I think deserves to be front and center for all of us: how effectively are we using technology in our own presentations?

You may not be incorporating a virtual coach or other futuristic elements in your speeches, talks, and lectures. But are you using the technology available today as an effective tool of audience engagement and interest?

Voice-overs similar to the simulated virtual coach in this presentation; embedded videos; and even customized talking avatars can be part of your slide deck these days. If you're presenting remotely, the combination of the visuals of your slides and your voice expanding upon what your audience sees can be a winning combination. Today, you don't need a full-blown webinar to offer information to users worldwide, though that option certainly exists. Software and online platforms in a wide range of options and sophistication are available, and they're increasingly easy to learn and use.

And don't forget the beauty of low-tech! It's all at your fingertips, from flip charts and white boards to web cams, laptop mics, smartphones, high-def video cameras (smaller and cheaper than ever), and video and audio editing software.

So play around with any or all of it. You'll probably be amazed at the effects you can achieve cheaply and simply. It's all part of the requirement—more important now than ever before—to keep your audiences continually engaged.

100: A Four-Stage Rocket for Launching a Successful Webinar

Let's say you took the advice offered in Quick Tip #99 above and are giving a one-hour webinar. Your "vehicle" needs to generate enough lift to achieve escape velocity, right? To stay with that metaphor, you need a four-stage rocket for a successful mission that (1) describes things fully and powerfully, (2) directs viewers to the right landing zone, (3) generates enough forward thrust, and (4) communicates clearly in real time.

Stage One: Descriptive Power. Since you're not speaking in person to the webinar attendees, they are bereft of the rich array of visual clues you give when presenting. To compensate, you have to boost your vocal expressiveness. I recommend that you stand and move while you're speaking and that you use a headset with a microphone. Listeners will hear your body language (which amplifies what you're saying), and the headset will free you to gesture naturally.

Stage Two: Hitting the Target Zone. Viewers may be confused and miss the "target zone" of where you want them to look on your slides. With data-heavy slides in particular, webinar attendees may spend valuable time trying to coordinate what you're saying with what they're seeing. Make it easy for them by saying something like,

"If you look at the pie chart in the upper right, you'll notice…"

Stage Three: Forward Thrust. Nothing kills the buzz more at the start of a webinar than an initial slide that stays displayed for 15 minutes. Remember: a webinar is primarily visual. You need to move at a good clip through your visual selections, keeping things interesting while achieving forward thrust.

Stage Four: Keeping the Communication Channel Open. Webinars-as-monologues are deadly. Be sure to build in questions that you ask attendees; and carve out some time to address relevant or important queries. Even though you're presenting virtually, participants need to feel that your talk is a two-way street they can drive on as well. Never forget the multiple distractions that, minute by wicked minute, are seducing your webinar attendees away from you.

101: The Big Bang Theory of Public Speaking

This is a tale of two speakers, a universe apart.

Both were keynoters at the annual meeting of a professional association; and each was a scientist. The first keynote was ceremonial, while the second was visionary. But that doesn't explain why one speech reached escape velocity while the other never left the launch pad.

Actually, the speeches weren't the issue at all. The key factor was the ability of one presenter to connect with his audience, versus the speaker who stayed hidden behind the blast wall of his content.

In other words, it all had to do with performance.

So what did the second presenter, the successful one, know that the first speaker didn't? And how did he make a presentation with much denser information actually feel lighter and more engaging? As I listened to these speakers, I realized it all had to do with what I'm calling The Big Bang Theory of Public Speaking.

The Big Bang theory in cosmology, of course, says that the universe expanded from a massively dense condition in a single event, and that it continues to expand, with objects farthest from us accelerating away from us faster than anything closer. The older, rival Steady State theory, on the other hand, states that the universe remains unchanged from wherever it's observed, and the density of matter remains steady.

I realized that the audience at that annual meeting was experiencing a steady state with the first speaker. The content of his speech concerned the leadership of the association in the coming year. It might have been interesting; but his lulling, unexcited and unexciting delivery made the material seem commonplace, perfunctory, and uninspired. Truly, this was steady state speaking that needed a Big Bang to make it come alive!

So, to your own successful public speaking: Do you know how to talk to an audience, understanding how a conversational style adds to the relationship you build with listeners? In other words: is there *humanity* on display when you speak? How, for instance, will listeners grasp which points are truly important if not through your voice, eye contact, and the passion with which you speak?

In the steady state style of delivery, the content becomes a Sea of Tranquility. There are no soaring peaks or low-lying quiet valleys; and there's no urgency to anything. Even the speech with interesting content is neutralized and flattened. No relationship with the audience exists; and the speaker is a distant figure on a faraway planet seen only through a telescope.

How many of us do better than that by achieving actual *contact* with our audience, employing an easy natural style of delivery that still allows the important and exciting parts of our presentation to stand out? Relating to listeners in this way always matters more than your exact words, because reaching people is what you're there to accomplish.

A pair of speeches, then, equally accurate and timely and with valuable content. Yet these talks were entirely different in the only way that matters in the end, in terms of how powerfully they reached and moved people.

Chalk it up to evolving theories of how to connect with audiences in the vastness of the public speaking universe.

INDEX

PHOTO BY LYDIA GENARD

GARY GENARD is one of America's leading speech coaches. As an actor, he created The Genard Method to bring theater-based techniques to business leaders and other professionals with a need to influence audiences. Dr. Genard consults for corporations, governments, trade associations, and executives and leadership teams worldwide. He is the author of *Fearless Speaking: Beat Your Anxiety, Build Your Confidence, Change Your Life* and the weekly blog *Speak for Success!*

Connect with him on Twitter @GaryGenard
Learn more at GenardMethod.com